Touring the Flatiron:

Walks in Four Historic Neighborhoods

Touring the Flatiron:
Walks in Four
Historic Neighborhoods

Joyce Mendelsohn

New York Landmarks
Conservancy
1998

Design: The Oliphant Press, New York

Initial research was carried out in 1996 under the auspices of the 23rd
Street Association, Inc., Douglas E. Sarini, Chairman of the Board, Paul
D.Custer, President, Jane R. Crotty, Executive Director. Early funding
was provided by the Association, Meringoff Properties, Inc., Lisa
Sorace, Project Manager, and a Tourism Initiative Grant from the
Office of Manhattan Borough President, Ruth Messinger.

*Frontispiece: The Flatiron Building soon after construction in 1903 at the intersection
of 23rd Street, Broadway, and Fifth Avenue*

Contents

This publication was made possible by grants from:

Furthermore, the publication program
    of the J.M. Kaplan Fund
Metropolitan Life Foundation
New York Life Insurance Company
The Rudin Foundation
Union Square Cafe and Gramercy Tavern

Additional funding was provided by:
E.J. Audi/The Home of Stickley
Baruch College of the City University of New York
Buchbinder & Warren, LLC
Gramercy Park Hotel
Meringoff Properties, Inc.
Office of the Manhattan Borough President
Stribling-Wells & Gay
Toy Manufacturers of America, Inc.

Foreword

The Flatiron area is home to the New York Landmarks Conservancy, a private, not-for-profit organization dedicated to preserving, protecting, and reusing architecturally significant buildings. For the past 25 years the Conservancy has provided technical assistance, grants, and loans of more than $10 million to owners of hundreds of historic buildings throughout the city and state.

Since 1987, from our offices at Fifth Avenue and 21st Street in the Ladies' Mile Historic District, we have watched the Flatiron neighborhood blossom as old buildings are restored and new businesses occupy the revitalized blocks. Conservancy staff members take personal enjoyment from being in the midst of an area so rich in architectural and cultural history. It's a great place to work every day or to visit from time to time.

The Conservancy is grateful to its neighbor, the 23rd Street Association, Inc., which for some 70 years has helped merchants and residents improve the area. We were delighted when Jane R. Crotty, former Executive Director of the Association, came to us with the idea of publishing a guide and introduced us to Joyce Mendelsohn, who had begun to research the area. Ms. Mendelsohn transformed the concept into this book, the third volume in the *Conservancy Tours* series. It is a portal to past- and present-day Madison Square, Gramercy Park, Ladies' Mile, and Chelsea.

We are also very grateful to the institutions which helped fund this publication. They are listed to the left, on the page facing this one. This support is very much appreciated.

So, welcome to our neighborhood. We'll see you around—*Touring the Flatiron*.

Sincerely,

Peg Breen, *President*
New York Landmarks Conservancy

The second Madison Square Garden, designed by Stanford White, occupied the entire block stretching from Madison Avenue to Fourth Avenue between East 26th and East 27th Streets from 1890 to 1925.

Introduction

This is a book about neighborhoods and their complexities, buildings and their stories, continuity and change. It is about preserving buildings and historic districts for their architectural merit and, at the same time, penetrating facades to examine the deeper significance of structures, to connect buildings not only to their place, but also to their place in history. It is about giving new life to old buildings: a cable railway power station transformed into a high-tech college library, a warehouse and an auto-repair garage converted to a contemporary art center, a union headquarters remodeled as a residence for people living with AIDS.

The book is organized as a series of four walking tours, three of them within historic districts. They take you to points of historic, cultural, architectural, and literary interest and tell the stories of people and events connected to those places. Ideally these walks should be savored in small portions so that you can focus on the architecture, mull over the history, and experience the unique texture of each neighborhood. The tours will lead you to **Madison Square, Gramercy Park, Ladies' Mile,** and **Chelsea,** diverse neighborhoods linked together by 23rd Street. The cores of two neighborhoods are 19th-century models of planned communities. Two sites are related to the shaping of modern Christmas celebrations, and two others are memorials to the victims of the Holocaust. Several places are associated with some of America's greatest authors, including Edith Wharton, Herman Melville, O. Henry, and Stephen Crane. On these walks you will come across buildings in a variety of architectural styles ranging from a peaked-roof Federal corner house, to Greek Revival and Italianate row houses, Gothic Revival churches, an Italianate Quaker meetinghouse, now a synagogue, Beaux-Arts and neo-Renaissance office buildings, iron-fronted commercial palaces, early skyscrapers, and an Art Deco diner. You will find the works of such outstanding architects as Stanford White, Richard Upjohn, Cass Gilbert,

Calvert Vaux, Carrère and Hastings, and Henry J.
Hardenbergh.

The first tour of **Madison Square** will take you from
the transcendent Flatiron Building in and around Madison Square Park to see commemorative sculptures and
early skyscrapers. You will find the site where Madison
Square Garden originated, view the clock tower that was
once the tallest building in the world, and visit the tomb
of an heroic American general. The walk ends at
Theodore Roosevelt's birthplace, a rebuilt 19th-century
brownstone, open to the public.

The second walk will guide you around the elegant
enclave of town houses and venerable clubs surrounding
Gramercy Park. You will discover how several outstanding writers are connected to this neighborhood, see a
hotel favored by celebrities, a vintage neighborhood tavern, and the armory, where modern art burst on the
American scene in 1913.

As a third tour, you will discover the remarkable collection of newly-restored Victorian department stores on
Ladies' Mile, locate the city's most popular outdoor flea
market, and look behind commercial storefronts to discover former brownstone residences, one of them the
birthplace of Edith Wharton. Nearby you will encounter
an old Sephardic Jewish burial ground, and a desolate
church complex converted to a nightclub.

In a fourth walk, you will explore the mid-19th-cen-
tury historic center of old **Chelsea** with its restored row
houses, historic churches, and a cloistered seminary.
On the surrounding streets you will visit a legendary
hotel, stop by an Art Deco diner, see experimental theaters, new art galleries enlivening once-desolate blocks,
and a sports and entertainment facility housed in renovated piers.

10

At the turn of the century the winds generated at the corner of 23rd Street in front of the Flatiron Building lifted ladies' skirts daringly above their shoes, prompting policemen to urge onlookers to move on or, in the local idiom, "23 skiddoo." Now you are encouraged to move on with the help of these guided walks, to explore four of the most vibrant neighborhoods in the city, rich in history, architecture, commerce, and culture.

Madison Square Park looking north from East 23rd Street in 1899. At the right are the Home Office building of the Metropolitan Life Insurance Company and the first Madison Square Presbyterian Church. To the north, the tower of the second Madison Square Garden rises in back of the Appellate Division Courthouse. At the left stands the Fifth Avenue Hotel on the corner of 23rd Street.

Madison Square Neighborhood Walk

Introduction

The Madison Square neighborhood is defined by Madison Square Park at its center and the Flatiron Building at its heart. The park, with its varied collection of outdoor sculpture, is surrounded by an array of office towers where once stood lavish mansions, luxury hotels, and lively entertainment centers. The area was originally mapped as The Parade, a military outpost established in 1807 covering almost 240 acres from the present 23rd to 34th Streets between Third and Seventh Avenues and including the site of an earlier burial ground. Barracks and an arsenal were built on The Parade as part of the city's defense system against the British in anticipation of the War of 1812. By 1814 the area was reduced to approximately 90 acres and named Madison Square in honor of James Madison, a strong champion of the Bill of Rights, a leader in the drafting and ratification of the Constitution, and fourth president of the United States (1809-1817). When the present Madison Square Park, scaled down to 6.8 acres, officially opened on May 10, 1847, New York's mayor was a Whig named William V. Brady, the city's population numbered nearly half a million, and residential development stretched to Union Square. On the national scene, James Polk was president and the American flag flew with 29 stars.

Residential development, moving northward from Union Square, reached Madison Square by the mid-1850s when Italianate brownstone row houses and several large mansions were built facing the park. For the next 20 years the neighborhood around the square was the core of an aristocratic enclave, the birthplace of author Edith Wharton and President Theodore Roosevelt, and the childhood home of Winston Churchill's mother, Jennie Jerome.

The Fifth Avenue Hotel opened on the corner of West

23rd Street in 1859, invading a wealthy residential area. Given the proximity to the terminal of the New York, New Haven & Hartford Railroad and the growth of Madison Square as a center of social activity, other hotels soon followed, establishing Madison Square as a hotel district in the 1860s and 1870s.

After the Civil War, new prosperity fueled the growth of an entertainment district close to Madison Square as increasing commercialization forced many wealthy residents to move further northward. Expensive restaurants and theaters crowded into the neighborhood. Society banquets and grand balls attended by Vanderbilts, Belmonts, and other members of the wealthy classes were held in Delmonico's, on West 26th Street facing Madison Square Park, and other select establishments nearby. Financiers such as Jim Fisk and Jay Gould dined and gambled in elegant restaurants and exclusive clubs in the area. Lily Langtry, Lillian Russell, and Sarah Bernhardt performed for enthusiastic audiences in nearby theaters. During the day thousands of shoppers flocked to specialty shops and department stores on the neighboring streets of **Ladies' Mile.** (See the third tour.)

Theodore Dreiser captures the excitement of the "night's amusements" in the hotels and places of entertainment around Madison Square and the nightly ritual of a charity collection for the hundred or so homeless men waiting in the "bed line" on 26th Street and Fifth Avenue in *Sister Carrie*, his penetrating novel of New York in the 1890s.

Beginning in 1874 on the east side of the square Barnum's Hippodrome, then Gilmore's Garden, followed by the first Madison Square Garden occupied the train depot and sheds abandoned when the first Grand Central Depot was constructed on East 42nd Street in 1871. Circus acts, band concerts, light opera, and later, boxing tournaments and horse shows took place in the unheated structures. In 1890 the railroad facilities were replaced by Stanford White's glittering Madison Square Garden, offering a variety of entertainment in a spectacular pleasure-palace containing a vast arena, a theater and concert hall, a roof garden, and an elaborate tower.

Madison Square continued to flourish as the main hotel and entertainment center of the city until the early 1900s, when social activity headed north and business development transformed the area into an office district. In 1883 the Western Union Building went up on Fifth Avenue and 23rd Street. The Metropolitan Life Insurance Company (now MetLife) constructed the first of several buildings on Madison Square in 1893. The Flatiron Building, completed in 1903, became an instant symbol of the skyscraper age. In 1908 the Fifth Avenue Hotel was replaced by the Fifth Avenue Building, now the International Toy Center. Madison Square Garden came down in 1925 to make way for the New York Life Insurance Company building and the Jerome mansion was demolished in 1967 for construction of the New York Merchandise Mart. Today business is thriving with insurance companies, investment banking, advertising agencies, publishing houses, media and Internet companies, photographers, graphic designers, marketing groups, real estate firms, and up-scale restaurants located in the area along with wholesale showrooms for toys, holiday ornaments, and the tableware and gift industries. More than a dozen companies carry the Flatiron name including a business association, a magazine, and a major venture capitalist, as the historic Madison Square neighborhood reinvents itself as the Flatiron District.

The New York City Landmarks Preservation Commission has designated the following individual landmarks found on the Madison Square Walk:

- Sidewalk Clock, 200 Fifth Avenue (Hecla Iron Works, 1909)
- Flatiron Building (Daniel H. Burnham & Co., 1901-1903)
- Metropolitan Life Insurance Company Tower (Napoleon LeBrun & Sons, 1907-1909)
- Appellate Division Courthouse (James Brown Lord, 1896-1900)
- Charles Scribner's Sons (Ernest Flagg, 1893-1894)
- Theodore Roosevelt Birthplace (Reconstructed, Theodate Pope Riddle, 1920-1923)

The tour begins at
the sidewalk clock
in front of 200
Fifth Avenue
between West
23rd and West
24th Streets.

Tour

MS1 Sidewalk Clock (Hecla Iron Works, 1909). Before
wristwatches became popular in the 1920s, gentlemen
carried pocket watches, ladies wore jewelry timepieces,
and everyone else relied on street clocks. This ornate,
cast-iron sidewalk clock is one of the few remaining in
the city and replaced a similar clock in the same location.

*Hotels on Fifth Avenue
facing the western edge
of Madison Square in
1899. The Fifth
Avenue Hotel fills the
block from 23rd Street
to 24th Street. To the
north are the
Albemarle Hotel and
Hoffman House.*

MS2 This was the site of the **Fifth Avenue Hotel** (Griffith
Thomas & Son, 1856-1858) which stretched from West
23rd to West 24th Streets along Fifth Avenue. The six-
story, white marble-faced hotel offered such amenities
as one of New York's first passenger elevators, fireplaces
in every bedroom, and numerous private bathrooms.
Guests included foreign royalty, most notably the Prince
of Wales (in 1860), U.S. presidents, and newly-minted
millionaires. In its early years the Fifth Avenue Hotel,
with its opulently decorated rooms for dining and dancing, was the center of the city's aristocratic social scene,
but after the Civil War, as new fortunes were made, it
began to lose its exclusivity.

    The hotel was long known as a Republican stronghold. In the 1890s Party boss Senator Thomas Platt presided over the legendary "Amen Corner" off the lobby, crowded with his loyal followers. Commodore Vanderbilt and other financiers ignored Wall Street's daily closings by extending the trading day well into the night at meetings in the hotel.

The Fifth Avenue Hotel was demolished in 1908 and replaced by **200 Fifth Avenue** (Maynicke & Franke, 1908-1909). Originally called the Fifth Avenue Building, it has been the headquarters of the toy industry in America since 1925 and was renamed the International Toy Center. The massive, 14-story limestone neo-Renaissance structure is linked by a skywalk to 1107 Broadway across West 24th Street. With more than one million square feet, the Toy Center houses showrooms and sales offices of leading toy and holiday decoration manufacturers, attracting 20,000 wholesale buyers to the district annually. A plaque with a history of the site can be found to the left of the arched entrance.

Walk to the north-west corner of Fifth Avenue and West 23rd Street.

MS3 186 Fifth Avenue stands directly across West 23rd Street. The handsome, seven-story red brick former Western Union Building, (Henry J. Hardenbergh, 1883) is a lesser known work of the eminent architect of the Dakota Apartments and the Plaza Hotel. It is one of the early office buildings in the area, predating the Flatiron Building by 20 years. This was a neighborhood branch, transmitting messages a distance of 2.5 miles in pneumatic tubes extending under Broadway to the downtown Western Union headquarters. The picturesque Queen Anne building remains remarkably intact above the ground floor. Note the decorated white terra-cotta panels and the company name in the West 23rd Street facade.

Cross Fifth Avenue to the traffic island.

MS4 The **Flatiron Building** (Daniel H. Burnham & Co., attributed to Frederick P. Dinkelberg, designer, 1901-1903) stands at 175 Fifth Avenue. With its dramatic form and rhythmic facade, it is recognized internationally as a skyscraper symbol of New York. The building was shaped to fit the triangular island centered in the cross-streams of traffic on Fifth Avenue, Broadway, and

Looking south from 24th Street to the Flatiron Building at the intersection of 23rd Street, with Broadway at the left and Fifth Avenue at the right, c. 1920.

23rd Streets. At first it was known as the Fuller Building after its owner and builder, the George A. Fuller Company. But after New Yorkers, intrigued by its wedge shape, began calling it "The Flatiron," the popular name was officially adopted. Of particular concern to its engineers was the need for various types of wind bracing to strengthen the unusually-shaped 21-story structure standing on such an exposed site. Gusts at the narrow-angled 23rd Street end gave rise to the colloquial expression "23 skiddoo" when police hustled away oglers hoping for a glimpse of a female ankle exposed by the wind.

Above the three-story limestone base much of the undulating midsection is clad in richly-decorated white terra cotta. Look for sculpted faces, lions' heads, foliage, and other French Renaissance-style ornament in the intricately detailed facade. A heavy projecting cornice crowning the building emphasizes its striking triangular form. The Flatiron has been compared to the prow of an ocean liner, an effect reinforced by the ground-floor glass-and-metal enclosure jutting out at the base of the building.

Contrary to popular lore, the 307-foot structure was not the first skyscraper in New York and was never the world's tallest. The Flatiron was built during the first generation of steel-skeleton-framed skyscraper construction in the city and enhanced the prestige of Madison Square as a developing office district. Early occupants included several publishers, and the tradition continues today with St. Martin's Press a tenant in the building.

Turn around and look up at the twin-globed **cast-iron lamppost** on the traffic island. By the 1890s ornamental electric lampposts along Fifth Avenue began replacing gas lamps. Fewer than 80 historic cast-iron lampposts survive in the city but three of them, all dating from the turn of the century, are within sight: this one, one diagonally across on the corner of West 23rd Street and Fifth Avenue, and another to be found directly across Broadway on the corner of East 23rd Street.

Cross Broadway and look across East 23rd Street.

The west side of Broadway from 22nd Street to 23rd Street, c. 1899. The block will soon be demolished for construction of the Flatiron Building. The Heinz sign is painted on the side of the Hotel St. Germaine.

MS5 Madison Green (Philip Birnbaum, 1983), with its entrance at 5 East 22nd Street, is a 31-story luxury condominium with 424 apartments, many with splendid views overlooking Madison Square Park. At the time this upscale building opened, most residential development

19

A Bishop's Crook street light stands near the statue of William H. Seward, c.1910.

in the neighborhood was limited to loft buildings converted to apartments. The construction of Madison Green signaled a new level of residential distinction for Madison Square.

Turn around to view the seated statue.

MS6 The bronze statue of **William H. Seward** by sculptor Randolph Rogers, erected in 1876, honors a popular New York governor, U.S. senator, secretary of state, and trusted advisor to Abraham Lincoln. The often-repeated story that Rogers created this statue by using castings from his 1871 sculpture of Lincoln in Fairmount Park, Philadelphia, and topping it with a new head of Seward seems to be partially true. Since the sponsoring committee couldn't pay his full fee, Rogers apparently economized by recycling Lincoln's lanky body parts (although Seward was described by contemporaries as "small and slender") to lower his costs. The sculptor repositioned the arms and legs, changed some details of dress, and cut back the Emancipation Proclamation which Lincoln had held, perhaps transforming it to the purchase agreement of Alaska, which Seward negotiated with Russia in 1867.

20

MS7 Madison Square Park is bounded by East 26th Street on the north, East 23rd Street on the south, Madison Avenue on the east and Fifth Avenue and Broadway on the west. Its formal 1870 design of walkways and lawns by Ignatz Pilat and William Grant remains largely intact, enhanced by statuary, plantings, and the addition of a playground and dog run. The park is frequented by a mix of people who live, work and shop in the area and a grow-ing number of tourists from around the world. It is the scene of periodic sculpture installations and special events including summer concerts and seasonal celebrations. In 1986 the city committed funds for total revitalization of the park but work was completed only in its northern sec-tion due to lack of money. A recent infusion of funds by elected officials and continuing support by neighboring businesses promise a rosy future for the park.

Enter the park.

In several short stories O. Henry tells the tales of down-and-outers who slept in the park in the early 1900s. In "Cop and the Anthem," a falling leaf arouses Soapy from his frigid park bench to look for a way to spend winter in a warm jail. In the classic "A Madison Square Arabian Night," a homeless man is plucked from the "bed line" to dine with an affluent gentleman who wants to hear his story. (More about O. Henry on the **Gramercy Park Tour.**)

Turn right and walk to the black rectangles behind the statue.

MS8 Looking north to the center of the park you will see the **Star of Hope**, a five-pointed star mounted on a 35-foot metal pole set in an ornamental base. It was erected in 1916 with funds donated by Minnie Dwight to com-memorate America's first community Christmas tree. That tree, the inspiration of Dwight and fellow artist Orlando Rouland, was lit in Madison Square Park on Christmas Eve, 1912, as a gift to the less fortunate in the city. The tradition of lighting a Christmas tree in the park lives on with annual festivities sponsored by the 23rd Street Association, Inc. and the New York City Depart-ment of Parks and Recreation.

MS9 The minimalist sculpture **Skagerrak**, composed of three weathering steel cubic rectangles, tilting on the grass was designed by Antoni Milkowski. The 1972 sculpture is named for the waterway separating Norway, Denmark, and Sweden. Be sure to view the geometric forms from various angles.

MS10 Roscoe Conkling, congressman, U.S. senator, and influential Republican political leader, is memorialized in this 1893 bronze statue by John Quincy Adams Ward. Conkling fell victim to the Great Blizzard of 1888, collapsing in the storm near Union Square and later dying of pneumonia.

MS11 Across the street is the **Metropolitan Life Insurance Tower** (Napoleon LeBrun & Sons, 1907-1909). The

Continue walking along the path parallel to East 23rd Street to the next statue.

Turn left and begin walking up the path parallel to Madison Avenue. Stop opposite the tower at East 24th Street.

Madison Avenue looking north from East 24th Street, c. 1905. At the right, the spire of the first Madison Square Presbyterian Church (James E. Ware, 1854-1855), razed in 1906 for the Metropolitan Life Insurance Tower. Across East 24th Street is the second Madison Square Presbyterian Church (Stanford White, 1904-1906), demolished in 1929 for the North Building of Metropolitan Life. Visible to the left is the Appellate Division Courthouse and the tower of the second Madison Square Garden.

company, now MetLife, was founded on lower Broadway in 1868. In 1893 the firm moved to new headquarters at One Madison Avenue on the corner of East 23rd Street. The architects of the original building later designed this adjacent 50-story, white marble Venetian belltower modeled after the 16th-century soaring Campanile in St. Mark's Square. At 700 feet it claimed the title of world's tallest from the Singer Tower (Ernest Flagg, 1908; demolished, 1970) on lower Broadway, and held it until the completion of the Woolworth Building (Cass Gilbert, 1913). The earlier Home Office building was replaced with the present corner building (D. Everett Waid, 1953-1957). In the next decade the tower was modernized (Lloyd Morgan and Eugene V. Meroni, 1960-1964), but its monumental clock faces, pyramidal top, cupola, chime, and shining gilded lantern were left intact.

The Metropolitan Life Insurance Tower, nearing completion in 1908, stands next to the earlier Home Office building. To the left is the second Madison Square Presbyterian Church.

MetLife was a pioneer in providing social services along with sales, producing health-related literature and establishing a Visiting Nurse Service for its policyholders. In the late 1940s the company built Stuyvesant Town and Peter Cooper Village (Irwin Claven and Gilmore Clarke), a development with more than 11,000 middle-income apartments in 110 red-brick buildings stretching from First Avenue to the FDR Drive, between East 14th and East 23rd Streets.

MS11a MetLife's immense limestone building **Eleven Madison** (Harvey Wiley Corbett and D. Everett Waid, 1929-1950) was originally known as its North Building. Planned as a 100-story tower, it could have been the world's tallest building, but with the onset of the Depression the building was capped at its present 29 stories. Erected in three stages with 2.2 million square feet of space, it occupies the entire block from East 24th to East 25th Streets, Madison Avenue to Park Avenue South. The modernist architects created an impressive Art Deco

Continue walking along the path. Stop facing Madison Avenue between East 24th and East 25th Streets.

masterwork featuring four arcaded corner entrances. Its massive bulk is animated by setbacks and angled walls above ornament in low relief. After a $300 million redesign of the interior and restoration of the exterior (Haines Lundberg Waehler, 1994-1997), MetLife leased more than 1.6 million square feet to the financial group Credit Suisse First Boston Corporation, bringing in a workforce of over 3,000. Other new tenants include Price Waterhouse and Emanuel Ungaro.

Around the turn of the century Madison Square lost its glow as the entertainment center of the city as extravagant hotels and restaurants were replaced by restrained loft and office buildings. After decades of gastronomic deprivation, fine dining is returning to the square with plans to develop high-quality restaurants in the vast ground floor and mezzanine spaces of Eleven Madison. In June 1997 Danny Meyer, an owner of Gramercy Tavern and Union Square Cafe, signed a 20-year lease for over 21,000 square feet of space for two restaurants facing the park (Peter Bentel, designer). The restaurants, Eleven Madison Park and Tabla, are expected to open in late summer, 1998. Similar space on the Park Avenue South side of the building will be occupied by another top-notch restaurant.

Look for a tablet in the ground in front of a large oak tree facing Eleven Madison.

MS12 Madison Avenue did not appear in the 1811 street plan, which emphasized access to the waterfronts and laid out closely spaced east-west streets while limiting the number of those running north and south. It was not until 1836 that the avenue was opened and named in honor of James Madison, who had died that year. This **pin oak tree** was brought from Montpelier, Madison's Virginia estate, and planted in 1936 to commemorate the centennial of the opening of Madison Avenue.

Take a close look at the soaring vaulted corner entrance of Eleven Madison with its splendid Art Deco ironwork.

Exit the park at East 25th Street. Cross Madison Avenue to the southeast corner of East 25th Street.

MS13 The **Appellate Division Courthouse** of the Appellate Division of the Supreme Court of the State of New York, First Judicial Department (James Brown Lord,

1896-1900), graces the northeast corner of Madison Avenue and East 25th Street. Preservation history was made here in December 1975 when the court upheld the constitutionality of the Landmarks Law, rejecting arguments by Penn Central that the New York City Landmarks Preservation Commission's denial of permission to build a tower over Grand Central Terminal was unconstitutional. The decision, upheld by the U.S. Supreme Court in 1978, was a significant victory for the preservation movement nationwide.

The courthouse, faced in white marble and influenced by designs of the Italian Renaissance architect Andrea Palladio, is a brilliant union of architecture, art and the law. One third of the total construction budget of close to $650,000 was allocated by the architect for paintings and statuary. Take the time to view the ancient legal luminaries that rule the roofline as well as the other sculptural groupings.

Cross East 25th Street.

The building, whose exterior and first floor interior are designated landmarks, is open to the public weekdays. In the entrance hall and courtroom are allegorical murals by almost a dozen different artists, depicting the history and wisdom of the law along with other judicial themes. The splendid furniture and woodwork were designed by the renowned firm of Herter Brothers. Ask the guard for a brochure that describes the building and identifies the artists. Be sure to see the courtroom with its exceptional stained-glass dome and windows by Maitland Armstrong. Glass cases in the lobby contain exhibits of historical documents.

Walk north on Madison Avenue to the end of the courthouse.

MS14 The **Memorial to the Victims of the Injustice of the Holocaust** (Harriet Feigenbaum, 1990), is a six-sided marble half-column which rises 27 feet above a 9.5 foot base on the north section of the wall of the courthouse extension (Rogers & Butler, 1951-1954) facing Madison Avenue. The sculptor symbolized the horror of the Holocaust with images of flames carved into the shaft above an aerial view of the death camp at Auschwitz. The inscription on the Memorial reads "Indifference to Injustice is the Gate to Hell."

Walk to East 26th
Street. Cross
Madison Avenue
to the corner of the
park.

MS15 Directly across the street at 41 Madison Avenue, is
the sleek International Style **New York Merchandise Mart**
(Emery Roth & Sons, 1974). The slender, 23-story building broke the line of traditional masonry buildings surrounding the park and introduced glass curtain-wall skyscraper design to Madison Square. The building houses
wholesale showrooms of china, crystal, silver, and glassware for the table-top market.

MS15a The **Jerome Mansion** stood on the site of this
modernist building. Built in 1859, it was the family residence of financier and sportsman Leonard Jerome and
childhood home of Jennie Jerome, who became Lady
Randolph Churchill, mother of British Prime Minister
Winston Churchill. The opulent French Second Empire
residence later housed a series of private clubs culminat-
ing with the Manhattan Club, a meeting place for such
Democratic notables as Grover Cleveland, Franklin Roosevelt, and Alfred E. Smith. Although designated a landmark in 1965 to prevent its demolition, after a two-year
effort failed to find a purchaser, the owners were permit-
ted in 1967 to raze the venerable mansion to make way
for the present glass tower.

MS16 **50 Madison Avenue** (Aspinwall & Owen, 1896),
across East 26th Street on the northwest corner of Madison Avenue, is a small office building in the form of an
Italian Renaissance palazzo. It was built for the American
Society for the Prevention of Cruelty to Animals, char-
tered in 1866 as the first humane society in America.

MS17 The **New York Life Insurance Company Building**
(Cass Gilbert, 1925-1928) stands diagonally across
Madison Avenue, occupying the block from East 26th to
East 27th Streets, Madison Avenue to Park Avenue South.
Its esteemed architect, Cass Gilbert, is well known for his
designs for the U.S. Custom House and Woolworth
Building in lower Manhattan. The distinguished lime-
stone building with Renaissance-inspired detailing is
crowned with a striking gilded pyramid which casts a
glow over Madison Square at night. New York Life

New York Life Insurance Company headquarters shortly after completion in 1928 seen from Madison Square Park. The small building to the right is the former Jerome Mansion.

received a Merit Citation Award from the New York Landmarks Conservancy after the pyramid was restored, re-tiled, and illuminated in 1995.

One of the oldest life insurers in the country, New York Life was founded in 1845 on Wall Street and later moved to lower Broadway. By 1860 the firm had established branches nationwide and had $3 million worth of policies in force. The company left its downtown headquarters at 346 Broadway (extant) and arrived on Madison Square in 1928. New York Life is the nation's fourth largest life insurance company by revenue, offering a full range of life insurance and financial products, and the sponsor of several urban housing developments.

Cross Madison Avenue and East 26th Street. Walk to the arched entrance for a closer look at the New York Life Insurance building.

View the splendid bronze gates and elegant entryway. During the week it is possible to enter the impressive marble lobby with its gilded ceilings and handsome hanging lamps, acclaimed as one of the great classical interior spaces in the city. A plaque to the left of the entrance describes the history of the site.

The first Madison Square Garden, c. 1880.

MS17a Madison Square Garden originated here. From 1837 to 1871 freight sheds of the New York & Harlem Railroad and a passenger depot of the New York, New Haven & Hartford Railroad occupied the site. After Commodore Vanderbilt opened the first Grand Central Depot on East 42nd Street in 1871, the abandoned train station was leased to P.T. Barnum, who created a circus arena in the unheated structure. Barnum's Hippodrome later became Gilmore's Garden, presenting evangelical meetings, band concerts, dog shows, and horticultural displays. In 1879 William H. Vanderbilt, son of the Commodore, reclaimed the lease and reopened with the name Madison Square Garden, an athletic arena turing mainly horse shows and prizefights.

In 1889 the first Madison Square Garden was demolished and replaced a year later by the palatial second Garden, designed by Stanford White. The architect's showpiece was an elaborately ornamented, dazzling structure of yellow brick and white Pompeian terra cotta with a splendid marble entrance on Madison Avenue recalling the Paris Opera. An impressive colonnade of Roman arches spanned Madison Avenue and extended into the sidestreets. The soaring 325-foot tower, completed in

The second Madison Square Garden with the Manhattan Club (in the former Jerome Mansion) draped with flags and bunting for the Democratic National Convention in June 1924. On the 103rd ballot delegates nominated John W. Davis, who was defeated by Calvin Coolidge in November.

The statue of Diana atop the tower of Madison Square Garden rotated in the wind and attracted considerable attention from crowds below.

1891, was modeled after the Giralda of Seville Cathedral. It was designed with a series of highly decorated loggias and originally topped by an eighteen-foot weathervane, *Diana* by Augustus Saint-Gaudens.

The thin-sheeted copper figure, finished with a delicate gold leaf was supported by a wrought-iron skeleton on ball-bearings that enabled the hunting goddess to rotate with the wind. After both the architect and sculptor realized that the first *Diana* was too big for the tower, it was replaced by a smaller version that stood 13 feet. The first sculpture was shipped to Chicago to adorn the Agricultural Building (McKim, Mead & White) at the 1893 World's Columbian Exposition. It may have been destroyed in an Exposition fire or survived and modified as "Progress" for the Tower Building of Montgomery Ward that was dismantled in 1947. The second *Diana* was removed from Madison Square Garden prior to that building's demolition. The statue languished in a warehouse for seven years before being presented by the New York Life Insurance Company to the Philadelphia Museum of Art, where it is on exhibit today. A gilt bronze half-size model, cast in 1928, can be seen in the American Wing of the Metropolitan Museum of Art.

Madison Square Garden occupied the block from Madison Avenue to Fourth Avenue between West 26th and West 27th Streets from 1890 to 1925. In its early years Madison Square Garden was acclaimed along with Central Park and the Brooklyn Bridge as one of the treasures of New York, and was celebrated as the leading entertainment center of the city. It boasted an amphitheater with a capacity of 8,000 and a 1,500-seat concert hall. It was the scene of elaborate entertainments, exhibitions, political rallies, sports competitions, and theatricals. Perhaps the Garden's most memorable drama was the real-life murder of architect Stanford White on the Roof Garden in 1906 by Harry K. Thaw, the crazed husband of former showgirl Evelyn Nesbit, an earlier flame of the architect.

Return to the park. Enter and walk a few steps to the statue.

MS18 This bronze portrait figure of **Chester Alan Arthur** by sculptor George Edwin Bissell was erected in 1899.

Arthur, vice-president in the Republican administration of James Garfield, became the 21st president of the United States after Garfield's assassination. He was awakened before dawn on September 20, 1881, to take the oath of office in the parlor of his brownstone row house nearby at 123 Lexington Avenue. That building, although altered, survives with a plaque in the entrance marking the historic event.

Continue walking along the path to the next statue.

MS19 The **Farragut Monument** by Augustus Saint-Gaudens, with its curved pedestal-bench by Stanford White, is acknowledged as a masterpiece of American public sculpture. Dedicated in 1881, this was Saint-Gaudens' first major work and marked the beginning of years of creative collaboration between sculptor and architect. It honors Admiral David Glasgow Farragut, Union fleet commander and Civil War hero, and recalls his stirring command, "Damn the torpedoes! Full speed ahead."

Farragut is depicted as a courageous figure, his coat blowing in the wind as he defies the elements and resolutely stands watch on the bridge of his ship. The realistic sculpture stands atop the more abstract relief carvings on the pedestal. The Admiral's sword stands upright in the waves of a sea inhabited by the symbolic female figures of Courage and Loyalty. Details of Farragut's life are inscribed in the ocean currents rippling over graceful dolphins at the corners of the pedestal, which is firmly anchored to a pebbled base recalling a shoreline. Look for a bronze crab embedded in the pebbles inscribed with the names of the sculptor and the architect . The free-flowing, organic style of the stone carving is said to be the first public appearance of the Art Nouveau style in America.

MS20 The **Worth Monument** marks the grave of Major General William Jenkins Worth, a hero of the Mexican War (Fort Worth, Texas, and Worth Street in lower Manhattan bear his name). After his death in San Antonio in 1849, his body was brought back to New York, his home state, and placed in a vault at Greenwood Cemetery in Brooklyn until his remains were interred

Enjoy a walk through the park. Then exit at East 25th Street on the west side of the park. Cross to the obelisk in Worth Square where Broadway and Fifth Avenue merge near 25th Street.

An elaborate gaslight illuminates Fifth Avenue at 24th Street. At right, the arm and torch of the Statue of Liberty, exhibited in Madison Square Park for six years beginning in 1876 in a campaign to raise funds to cast the statue and construct the base. At left, the Worth Monument.

here in 1857. The 51-foot granite obelisk, designed by James Goodwin Batterson, is ornamented with four carved bands listing significant battles in Worth's career. On the south face a sculptural grouping of 19th century weapons appears above the seals of the City and State of New York. Below, a bronze high relief depicts General Worth with raised sword on a rearing horse. On the iron fence surrounding the monument (cast in the foundry of J.B. & W.W. Cornell) is a series of ornamental swords, replicas of a dress sword awarded by New York to General Worth for his distinction in battle. The detailing includes miniature helmets topping the sword handles and oak leaves entwined in the fence.

Walk to the southern tip of Worth Square. Cross back to the park (carefully, at the crosswalk). Walk south, alongside the park, to the flagpole at East 24th Street.

The rectangular structure directly in back of the monument leads to Water Tunnel Number 1, completed in 1917, a water supply facility administered by the city's Department of Environmental Protection.

MS21 The **Eternal Light**, with its star-shaped lamp atop the flagpole, was designed by architect Thomas Hastings who, with partner John Carrère, designed the New York Public Library on Fifth Avenue. The memorial was

erected in 1918 and lit on November 11, 1923. It honors military heroes of World War I and is inscribed with the names of the battlefields on which they fought. In 1976 the original 120-foot, Oregon pine pole was replaced with a sturdier one made of steel.

By the 1890s tall office and loft buildings, many in the Beaux-Arts and neo-Renaissance styles, began to dominate Fifth Avenue between 14th and 23rd Streets. Today these splendid buildings house a wide range of companies in the publishing, advertising, and communications industries. Trendy stores in retail space on the ground floor level attract a steady stream of shoppers. (See the beginning of the **Madison Square** and **Ladies' Mile** tours for more on the Flatiron and other buildings visible from this vantage point.)

MS22 170 Fifth Avenue (Robert Maynicke, 1897-1898), with its gilded, octagonal dome, lights up the southwest corner of West 22nd Street. The Sohmer Piano Company was an early tenant, with offices and showrooms here. Today the slender, 13-story Beaux-Arts office building is filled with companies in publishing and the graphic arts.

Workmen repairing the Eternal Light in Madison Square Park, November, 1973.

Continue walking south alongside the park. Cross East 23rd Street and then cross Broadway. Walk to the Fifth Avenue side of the Flatiron Building.

Look south down Fifth Avenue.

Cross Fifth Avenue and walk to the northwest corner of West 22nd Street.

Walk down Fifth Avenue to the middle of the block between West 22nd and West 21st Streets.

MS23 The former Mortimer Building (Griffith Thomas, 1861-1862) at **935-939 Broadway** is diagonally across Fifth Avenue on the southeast corner, extending to Broadway. Its facades on both major streets are virtually identical. Although the design of the five-story Italianate brownstone building suggests a mansion or private club, this was an early commercial invader with ground-floor stores and offices above.

MS24 The elegant, six-story building at 155 Fifth Avenue is **Rapaport House,** originally Charles Scribner's Sons (Ernest Flagg, 1893-1894). One of America's pre-eminent publishers, Scribner's numbered among its authors Robert Louis Stevenson, Rudyard Kipling, and renowned American authors Henry James, Edith Wharton, Ernest Hemingway, F. Scott Fitzgerald, and Thomas Wolfe. Architect Ernest Flagg's training at the École des Beaux Arts is evident in the design of this elegant, Parisian-influenced structure. Flagg, a brother-in-law of Charles Scribner, later designed homes for various members of the family, as well as the former Scribner building at 597 Fifth Avenue. The letter "S" can be found in the iron ovals of the fourth floor balcony. Roman numerals above mark the company's founding in 1846 in lower Manhattan, as well as the date of this building. Since 1974 it has been occupied by the United Synagogue of Conservative Judaism, an association of Conservative congregations in North America, and has been renamed Rapaport House.

MS25 **141 Fifth Avenue** (Robert Maynicke, 1896-1900) is crowned by an imposing dome over the curved corner of the twelve-story Beaux-Arts building on the southeast corner of East 21st Street. Originally the Merchants Central Building, it was designed for stores, offices and lofts; one of the current occupants is the New York Landmarks Conservancy.

Continue walking down Fifth Avenue to West 20th Street. Cross Fifth Avenue to the northeast corner.

MS26 Two impressive office buildings stand on the west side of Fifth Avenue at the corners of West 20th Street. On the northwest corner is **156 Fifth Avenue** (Rowe &

34

Baker, 1894-1895), formerly known as the Presbyterian Building, with its dramatic Romanesque Revival entranceway. Picturesque dormers animate the roofline of this twelve-story building. At the turn of the century the offices of noted architects were to be found in the neighborhood. James Baker (the architect of this building), Albert Gottlieb, York and Sawyer, and the New York Chapter of the American Institute of Architects were all located here. The firm of McKim, Mead & White occupied the entire fifth floor of No. 160 next door.

MS27 **150 Fifth Avenue** (Edward H. Kendall, 1888-1890) on the southwest corner, is a red brick and white stone Romanesque Revival structure . Originally the Methodist Book Company, the nine-story building contained offices, printing presses, and a chapel. Architects Edward Hale Kendall (who designed the building) and Bruce Price occupied offices here. At the turn of the century this stretch of Fifth Avenue was known as "Paternoster Row," an allusion to the many religious institutions located between 16th and 23rd Streets (the *paternoster* is a common name for the Lord's Prayer).

Cross East 20th Street. Turn left and walk east on the south side of East 20th Street.

MS28 Two relics, by unknown architects, of a mid-19th-century residential neighborhood survive on the north side of East 20th Street. **No. 5** (1852-1853), a Renaissance Revival stable, and **No. 11** (1852-1853), an Italianate row house, were both converted to commercial use nearly 100 years ago.

Continue walking to Broadway.

(*Buildings further south on Broadway are described near the end of the* **Ladies' Mile** *walk.*)

Cross Broadway. Continue walking along East 20th Street.

MS29 A flag marks 28 East 20th Street, the **Theodore Roosevelt Birthplace National Historic Site** (Theodate Pope Riddle, 1920-1923). This is a meticulous reconstruction of the 1848 brownstone in which America's 26th president was born on October 27, 1858. The socially prominent Roosevelt family acquired the original in 1854 and lived in it for almost 20 years. In 1872, as businesses moved into the neighborhood, the

President Theodore
Roosevelt, c. 1905.

Roosevelts joined the northward exodus of the wealthy
and moved to West 57th Street. Although the original
brownstone was demolished in 1916, a twin survived at
No. 26 and was used as a model for the reconstruction.
The three-story house has a high stoop above a basement
and is capped by a mansard roof. Surmounting the
square-headed windows and rectangular doorway are
hooded moldings in the Gothic Revival style. One of
America's first female architects, Theodate Pope Riddle,
designed the memorial. The twin, No. 26, was demolished to make room for an adjoining museum, also
designed by Riddle.

Although debilitated by asthma as a boy, Roosevelt

overcame his infirmities and led a life of adventure, first as a cowboy in the Dakotas, then as a colonel of the Rough Riders in Cuba, and as a hunter and naturalist on several continents. He spent nearly 40 years in active political life, beginning at 23 when he was elected to the New York State Legislature. Vice-president under William McKinley in 1901, he became president that year after McKinley's assassination. Roosevelt was elected President in 1904 and received the Nobel Peace Prize in 1906 for his efforts in ending the Russo-Japanese War. In 1919 the former president died at Sagamore Hill, his house in Oyster Bay, Long Island.

Take advantage of the opportunity to visit the home of one of America's most distinguished presidents, where you will see period furnishings and experience the lifestyle of an affluent 19th-century New York family. The house and museum, operated by the National Park Service, are open to the public for a small fee, Wednesday through Sunday, 9:00 A.M. to 5:00 P.M. The last tour of the house is at 4:00 PM.

Gramercy Park looking northeast from East 20th Street, 1905.

Gramercy Park
Neighborhood Walk

Introduction

A sense of order and tranquility pervades Gramercy Park, a residential square developed in the mid-19th century from farmland. The area was originally part of a larger tract purchased in 1651 from the Dutch West India Company by Peter Stuyvesant, fourth Director General of New Amsterdam. In 1674 Stuyvesant's widow, Judith, deeded a portion of the land to Frans Bastiansen, a freed slave, possibly to provide a buffer zone against Indian attack. The property reverted to the Stuyvesant family after Bastiansen's death, and in 1761 was acquired by James Duane (mayor of New York, 1784-89) along with adjoining acreage. Duane established Gramercy Farm, taking the name from Crommessie, in Dutch "crooked knife," a brook that cut through the property.

Samuel B. Ruggles, a lawyer with an interest in real estate, bought the 20-acre Duane farm for residential development in 1831. He laid out 66 building lots; that number was reduced to 62 lots with the opening of Lexington Avenue and Irving Place in 1833. As an amenity Ruggles set aside 42 additional central lots as a private park to provide a shared front yard for the exclusive use of the property owners around the square. He enclosed Gramercy Park with an iron fence and ornamental locked gates, and deeded the park to five trustees. Ruggles used as his model a similar private park called Hudson Square, later known as St. John's Park, which had been laid out by Trinity Church in 1803 in what is now Tribeca. That square was destroyed in 1869 when Trinity sold the property to Commodore Vanderbilt for railroad facilities.

In the 1830s the public squares laid out in the Commissioners' plan of 1811 in remote regions of upper Manhattan existed only on maps. New Yorkers in search of fresh air and greenery in lower Manhattan frequented the Battery, Bowling Green, and City Hall Park. Washington Square Park, Tompkins Square, Union Square, and Stuyvesant Square further uptown were all public parks. In 1832 the city's Board of Aldermen exempted Gramercy Park from taxation and assessment, deeming private squares a benefit to the public, a view upheld in 1911 by the Appellate Division of the New York State Supreme Court and later affirmed on appeal. Although there are numerous communal private gardens in the city, some tucked behind row houses as in Turtle Bay, others within apartment complexes such as London Terrace (see the **Chelsea Walk**), they are hidden away and do not provoke controversy. But Gramercy Park, the city's only private park in open sight, arouses conflicting reactions from the public ranging from appreciation and longing to astonishment and resentment.

Ruggles sold the building lots with restrictive covenants, prohibiting commercial enterprises and requiring property owners to build substantial brick or stone dwellings set back from the street. By the 1840s Gramercy Park emerged as a fashionable center for some of New York's wealthiest families. Although most of the original brick and brownstone, Greek Revival and Italianate row houses have been replaced or reconstructed, many remain close to their original form. Two brownstone houses of worship remain standing, the 1846 Gothic Revival Calvary Church designed by James Renwick Jr. and the former Friends Meeting House by King and Kellum, presently the Brotherhood Synagogue, built in the Italianate style in 1859. Several of the original houses on the south side of the park were altered in the 1880s. Two row houses were unified with a new front in the Victorian Gothic style by Calvert Vaux for the Samuel Tilden mansion, now the National Arts Club. Stanford White redesigned the large Gothic Revival brownstone residence next door for The Players, a private club founded by Edwin Booth. White also renovated and enlarged No. 19 on the corner of Irving Place for industrialist Stuyvesant Fish and his wife Marian. That mansion was restored to its former glory in the 1940s by publicist Benjamin Sonnenberg and continues to be a private residence. The nine-story Gramercy, an early co-op apartment house, rose on the site of a hotel, the Gramercy Park House, on the east side of the square in 1883. It was followed in 1910 by a 12-story apartment house at No. 36 next door. After construction of the Gramercy Park Hotel and several apartment houses in the 1920s, high-rise buildings dominated the north side of the square.

The **Gramercy Park Historic District** was designated in 1966 by the newly-formed New York City Landmarks Preservation Commission and extended in 1988. The landmark district includes the private park and portions of the surrounding residential neighborhood roughly from East 18th to East 21st Streets between Park Avenue South and Third Avenue. In 1996 Gramercy Neighborhood Associates proposed extending the historic district to include additional buildings within those borders, designation of a substantial number of individual structures as far north as East 23rd Street, and a new historic district centered on East 17th Street. Thanks to a campaign led by preservation activist Jack Taylor, the Commission recently designated the **East 17th Street/Irving Place Historic District**, Nos. 104-120 on the south side of East 17th Street between Irving Place and Union Square East, plus 47 and 49 Irving Place.

Tour

GP1 A row of substantial homes for the wealthy once lined the block where the hotel now stands. When Samuel Ruggles' daughter Ellen married lawyer George Templeton Strong in 1848, the couple received as a wedding present a mansion at **113 East 21st Street,** which Strong dubbed the "XXIst Street Palazzo." Strong kept voluminous diaries spanning almost 40 years, providing unrivaled insights and eye-witness accounts of 19th century life in New York, including such events as a U.S. Army encampment in Gramercy Park during the Draft Riots in the summer of 1863. A few doors to the east stood the first home of Strong's Columbia University classmate George Frederic Jones and Lucretia Rhinelander Jones, future parents of Edith Wharton.

The tour begins on the northwest corner of Lexington Avenue and Gramercy Park North (East 21st Street) next to the Gramercy Park Hotel.

Gramercy Park North, west of Lexington Avenue, 1905. Stanford White's corner home and several adjacent houses were replaced in 1924 by the Gramercy Park Hotel.

Cross to the
northern side of
the park.

GP1a In 1892 celebrated architect and bon vivant Stanford White and his wife Bessie Smith White leased their first home on Gramercy Park. It was a brownstone row house at **119 East 21st Street**, marked with a plaque with inaccurate dates. In the spring of 1898 the Whites rented a more spacious home, which they maintained until the architect's death in 1906, at **No. 121** on the northwest corner of Lexington Avenue and East 21st Street. White created a lavish interior for his collection of Oriental rugs, Gothic tapestries, Chinese vases, priceless books, Holbein portraits, and other art and antiques. Over the years Stanford White remodeled and redecorated several other houses for wealthy patrons around the park.

GP2 The Jones and White houses were among those razed when the 18-story **Gramercy Park Hotel** at 2 Lexington Avenue (Robert T. Lyons, 1924-1925, and addition, 1929-1930) was constructed. Several marble fireplaces from the Stanford White corner house were recovered and installed in suites in the new hotel. A few years after it opened the Joseph P. Kennedy family (including pre-teen John F. Kennedy) is said to have occupied an entire floor for several months. Over the years the hotel has attracted numerous celebrities such as Humphrey Bogart, who married his first wife, actress Helen Menken, here in 1926. James Cagney and his wife Billie were frequent diners at the restaurant while maintaining an apartment at 34 Gramercy Park. Irish actress Siobhan McKenna made the hotel her New York home, and the author and humorist S. J. Perelman was a long-term resident, dying in his room in 1979. The hotel continues to draw visitors from around the world with its old-world charm and Gramercy Park ambiance.

Along with every other building with windows facing the private park, the Gramercy Park Hotel is assessed for the upkeep of this privileged urban oasis. The original cost was $10 per lot. The current rate is $1,900 annually, with two keys allocated for each lot. As the hotel covers six lots, it holds 12 keys to the park. One day a year, usually the first Saturday in May, the park is open to the public.

Walk west alongside the park. Cross Gramercy Park West and walk toward the corner of Park Avenue South.

GP3 The brownstone Episcopal **Calvary Church** (James Renwick Jr., 1846-1847) occupies the northeast corner of East 21st Street and Park Avenue South. Renwick is the famed architect of Grace Church and later St. Patrick's Cathedral. He designed the Gothic Revival Calvary with twin wooden spires that, after weakening, were removed in the 1860s. Also by Renwick is a little Victorian Gothic Sunday school (1867, used today as a furniture thrift shop) adjoining the church on Park Avenue South. A collection of splendid stained-glass windows, a Tiffany mosaic fountain, and a particularly fine organ are to be found within the church.

The Rev. Edward Washburn (rector from 1865-1881) was the model for Dr. Ashmore in Edith Wharton's *The Age of Innocence*, as well as the father of Emelyn

Washburn, Edith's closest childhood friend. Prominent parishioners included the Roosevelt family, who lived nearby. Theodore was godfather to his brother Elliot's daughter, future First Lady Eleanor Roosevelt, who was baptized at home in 1884 by the rector of Calvary Church. The Rev. Stephen Garmey, vicar of Calvary Church and a strong supporter of historic preservation, is the author of *Gramercy Park: An Illustrated History of a New York Neighborhood*, the authoritative sourcebook on the area.

Retrace your steps back to the park. Walk along the western side of the park to the gate in the middle of the block.

Gramercy Park looking northeast, c. 1935.

GP4 Two memorials to **Samuel B. Ruggles**, both presented by his grandson, John Ruggles Strong, can be found near the west gate of the park. Embedded in the bluestone sidewalk is a commemorative tablet installed in 1875. Peer through the west gate into the park to see the small medallion head of Ruggles by Edmond T. Quinn, mounted on a Tennessee marble shaft designed by Charles I. Berg and erected in 1919. (Also in sight is a statue of Edwin Booth that we will reach shortly.)

The private park was first landscaped in 1838 when the trustees hired James Virtue to establish a border of privet along the inside of the iron fence. By the following year paths had been laid out and a variety of shrubs and trees planted. In 1916 Brinley & Holbrook, landscape architects and engineers, added perimeter flower beds, Norway Maples, Yellow Buckeyes, and Siberian Elms. Although the park's original formal design has been retained, the prim nature of the early ornamental square has evolved over the years into a lush garden of flowers and greenery. A long-range plan for improvement, commissioned by the Trustees in 1991 and developed by Quennell Rothschild Associates, calls for restoration of the iron fence and more informal plantings of perimeter borders and flowering trees.

GP5 a-c Despite the demolition or renovation of many of the earliest houses around Gramercy Park, several survive almost intact. Directly across the street, five brick houses, built between 1844 and 1850, form a harmonious row on the western edge facing the park. The Italiante row house with its Ionic portico at **No. 1** belonged to Dr. Valentine Mott, a respected physician and surgeon. **Nos. 3 and 4,** built in the Greek Revival style, are attributed to Alexander Jackson Davis, one of the city's leading pre-Civil War architects. They are outstanding for their lacy cast-iron verandas, railings, and balconies enlivened by anthemion (stylized honeysuckle) designs sprouting from the top of the porches. A pair of ornate iron lanterns flank the entrance to No. 4. Before Gracie Mansion became the official mayor's resi-

Row houses on Gramercy Park West, 1905.

dence in 1942, special lanterns marked the private homes of the city's mayors. James Harper, a founder of Harper & Brothers publishers, moved here in 1847 after his term as mayor (1844-1845) and brought his lamps with him.

Continue walking on Gramercy Park West. Stop at the corner of Gramercy Park South (East 20th Street).

GP6 10 Gramercy Park, diagonally across the street to the right, is a brownstone row house with a large glass skylight. From 1909 to 1929 this was the studio and home of painter and teacher Robert Henri. Henri was at the center of a group of painters called The Eight: Maurice Prendergast, John Sloan, William Glackens, George Luks, Everett Shinn, Ernest Lawson, Arthur B. Davies, and Henri. They were united in opposition to the rigid standards of academic painting. (More about this group at the 69th Regiment Armory, later in this tour.)

Turn left and walk a few steps.

GP7 The **National Arts Club** at No. 15 was formerly the home of Democratic reform politician Samuel J. Tilden. The original two mid-1840s row houses were remodeled (1881-1884) by British architect Calvert Vaux into this distinctive mansion. Vaux, who earlier collaborated with Frederick Law Olmsted in the creation of Central Park, designed the facade in a style inspired by John Ruskin, using stone in varied colors and naturalistic ornament of flora and fauna. Medallion heads of Shakespeare, Milton, Goethe, and other distinguished figures of literature and philosophy adorn the mansion. The architect also redesigned much of the interior, adding an elaborately gilded wood-paneled dining room, a vaulted central glass dome by Donald MacDonald, and stained-glass window panels by John LaFarge.

Tilden resigned as Governor of New York to run for president in 1876 against Rutherford P. Hayes. He won the popular vote but was subsequently denied victory by one electoral vote in what many historians consider the most infamous election dispute in American history. When Tilden, who never married, died ten years later he left the bulk of his estate to the Tilden Trust. A $2.2 million contribution from the Trust, along with Tilden's extensive library and the Astor and Lenox legacies, formed the nucleus of the New York Public Library, established in 1895.

The National Arts Club, founded in 1898, acquired the Tilden mansion in 1906. The "arts" embraced painting, sculpture, music, and literature. Early members included Theodore Roosevelt, Woodrow Wilson, and collectors Henry Clay Frick, Benjamin Altman, and J.P. Morgan. Among the artists were architect Stanford White, painters William Merritt Chase, George Bellows and Robert Henri, sculptors Augustus Saint-Gaudens, Frederick Remington, and Anna Hyatt Huntington (women have been members since 1906). The club is open only to members and their guests. Frequent art exhibits are accessible to the public in limited areas of the building.

GP8 Next door at No. 16 is **The Players**, a private club founded in 1888 by Edwin Booth, America's leading 19th-century Shakespearean actor. Booth formed The Players to raise the prestige of acting by providing a respectable setting where men of the theater could assemble

Interior of The Players, 1907.

with gentlemen of other professions. Civil War General William Sherman and celebrated author Mark Twain were early members. In recent years the star-studded roster has included Sir Laurence Olivier, Tony Randall, Christopher Reeve, and James Earl Jones. It was not until 1989 that this male bastion opened its doors to women. Among the first female members were Helen Hayes, Lauren Bacall, Lillian Gish, and Leontyne Price.

Booth purchased the 1840s Gothic Revival brownstone residence at No. 16 in 1887. He commissioned Stanford White, who waived his fee in exchange for a lifetime membership in the club, to design the renovations. The architect redesigned the interior and on the exterior left intact the original drip lintels on the upper floors, but added the present cornice graced with theatrical masks. White also altered the entranceway by adding an elaborate ironwork porch with splendid iron lanterns. Within the clubhouse, Booth established a library that holds unique materials relating to American and British theater history. It contains Booth's thousand-volume library, his collection of Shakespeare prompt-books, diaries, correspondence, and records of the Booth Theatre (see the **Ladies' Mile Tour**). On display is a copy of Booth's sorrowful letter addressed to the people of the United States after his brother, John Wilkes Booth, assassinated Abraham Lincoln. During the last five years of his life, Booth occupied a simply furnished third floor bedroom-sitting room facing the park which remains intact. Local legend holds that a thunderstorm dimmed the lights around Gramercy Park at the moment of Booth's death at midnight on June 7, 1893.

Although The Players is not open to the public, access to the Hampden-Booth Theatre Library is available by appointment for scholars, theater professionals, and students.

Continue walking alongside the park to Irving Place.

GP9 Look through the locked iron gates of Gramercy Park to the bronze life-size statue of **Edwin Booth** (Edmond T. Quinn, dedicated 1918) as Hamlet, his most celebrated role. To the right of the gate is a plaque describing the history of Gramercy Park.

Look across Gramercy Park South to the southeast corner of Irving Place.

GP10 The five-story brownstone mansion at **No. 19**, originally a small 1845 row house, was expanded and altered by Stanford White in 1887 for railroad magnate Stuyvesant Fish and his high-society wife Marian, known as Mamie. Fish was a descendant of Revolutionary War hero Nicholas Fish and his wife Elizabeth Stuyvesant, great-great-great-granddaughter of Peter Stuyvesant. The couple's son, Hamilton Fish, was the first of many prominent family members of that name. The rebuilt 37-room mansion with its grand white marble staircase and top-floor ballroom was the scene of extravagant parties hosted by Mamie Fish. As New York society moved northward, the Fish family left Gramercy Park in 1898 for a magnificent palazzo-style mansion at 25 East 78th Street designed by Stanford White.

This house began to decline and was broken up into small apartments. Public relations genius Benjamin Sonnenberg rescued the former mansion from decay and made it once more a splendid private residence. In 1931 Sonnenberg and his wife Hilda rented the first two floors of the run-down house, gradually expanding into other apartments. In 1945 they bought the entire house for $85,000 from Stuyvesant Fish Jr. and furnished it with an elaborate collection of antiques and artwork. Over the years the Sonnenbergs hosted spectacular parties with a mix of guests ranging from old money to show-business celebrities. After Sonnenberg's death in 1978, the house was acquired by Baron Walter Langer von Langendorff, owner of Evyan Perfumes, and in 1995 sold to fashion designer Richard Tyler.

In his time-travel novel *Time and Again,* Jack Finney graphically depicts life in Gramercy Park in 1883. His hero, Simon Morley, rents a room in a fictional boardinghouse at No. 19, an address that did not exist at that time. The corner mansion, presently No. 19, bore an Irving Place address in 1883.

Guests at a lavish ball at the Waldorf-Astoria in 1897. Stanford White is at the center and Mrs. Stuyvesant Fish is seated at right.

Cross Gramercy
Park South and
look down Irving
Place.

Along with the creation of Gramercy Park, Samuel
Ruggles was instrumental in laying out two new streets:
Lexington Avenue, named for the Revolutionary War
battle site and Irving Place, honoring the distinguished
author and diplomat Washington Irving. Irving, born in
lower Manhattan in 1783, became America's first internationally acclaimed writer and served as U.S. Minister to
Spain. In the early 1800s Irving identified New York
with two names that continue to be popular today. Writing in his satirical magazine *Salmagundi* (a spicy stew) in
1807, Irving described New York as "Gotham," referring to a 16th-century British folk tale, "Merry Tales of
the Mad Men of Gotham." In that story the sly people of
Gotham feigned madness to dissuade King John from
building a castle in their town. Another label that survives is "Knickerbocker," originally indicating New
Yorkers of Dutch descent. Irving popularized that allusion in his witty 1809 novel of life in New Amsterdam, *A
History of New York*, published under the pseudonym
Diedrich Knickerbocker. Variations on that name, still in
use, recall the city's Dutch heritage.

Walk down the
west side of Irving
Place. Stop in front
of No. 81.

GP11 Fanciful creatures in terra cotta enliven the brick
apartment house at **No. 81** (George Pelham, 1929-
1930).

Continue walking
down Irving Place.

Irving Place is appreciated by savvy New Yorkers as a
unique dining opportunity. Sandwiched between Park
Avenue South and Third Avenue, the charming street is
home to distinctive shops and restaurants. In warm
weather tables and chairs line the sidewalk for pleasant al
fresco dining.

Stop mid-block
between East 18th
and East 17th
Streets.

GP12 A plaque at **No. 55** marks the site of a rooming
house where author O. Henry, born William Sidney
Porter in 1862, lived in the spacious front parlor from
1903 to 1907. As a young man Porter worked as a bank
teller in Texas and was sent to prison for embezzlement.
Porter wrote short stories in jail and, after his three-year
term, emerged as a professional writer under the name
O. Henry. Porter was one of America's most prolific and
original short story writers. He lived on Irving Place at

the height of his career, while he worked under a contract with the N.Y. *Sunday World* to write one story a week for the paper's magazine section. He published more than 100 stories in the *World*, receiving $100 for each story.

GP13 Although an attractive plaque in front of **49 Irving Place** states that Washington Irving lived in this 1844 Italianate corner house, there is no documentation to prove that claim. But from 1892 until 1912 the three-story brick house was occupied by an extraordinary couple, Elsie de Wolfe, acknowledged as America's first professional interior decorator, and literary agent Elizabeth Marbury, who represented George Bernard Shaw and Oscar Wilde, among others. Coincidentally, Wilde

Cross East 17th Street to the southwest corner.

O. Henry lived for four years in the first-floor parlor at 55 Irving Place. The space was occupied by a restaurant, pictured here in 1936. Many of his stories are set in the rooming houses and bars within walking distance of Irving Place.

Daguerreotype of Washington Irving, c. 1855.

51

stayed next door at No. 47 in 1883 during a visit to America. The high-power couple was well-known in New York's intellectual and art circles and hosted memorable parties mixing society guests with artists and writers. De Wolfe rebelled against the heavy, dark clutter of Victorian interiors and with architect Ogden Codman Jr. (co-author with Edith Wharton in 1897 of *The Decoration of Houses*), refurbished the interior of this house based on design principles of harmony, proportion, and light. De Wolfe worked with McKim, Mead & White on the 1902 remodeling of the White House and designed for clients like industrialist Henry Clay Frick and the Duke and Duchess of Windsor. After World War I, de Wolfe and Marbury ended their relationship; de Wolfe later married a British diplomat, Sir Charles Mendl.

Elsie de Wolfe and Elizabeth Marbury lived together in the corner house at 49 Irving Place for 20 years.

GP14 Directly across Irving Place, on the southeast corner of East 17th Street, is an 1885 bronze bust of Washington Irving by Friedrich Beer. The sculpture first stood in Central Park and was later moved to Bryant Park. It was placed in front of **Washington Irving High School** (C.B.J. Snyder, 1911-1913) and rededicated in 1935. The school originally opened as Girls' Technical High School. Its list of famous students includes Whoopi Goldberg, Norma Kamali, Sylvia Sydney, and Claudette Colbert. The restrained exterior of the eight-story, brick and limestone building masks splendid interior spaces.

During school hours you can step inside through the arched entrance to see the baronial interior with its handsome woodwork, large fireplace inglenook, and series of murals by Barry Faulkner, as well as other works of art.

Look down Irving Place to the northeast corner of East 14th Street.

GP15 The **Consolidated Edison Company Building** (Henry J. Hardenbergh, 1910-1914), with its 26-story tower (Warren & Wetmore, 1926-1929), fills the block from East 14th to East 15th Streets, Irving Place to Third Avenue. The tower is topped by the "Tower of Light," a miniature temple, with clock faces on all four sides of the base, capped by a bronze lantern that is illuminated at night.

Utility companies have occupied a portion of this site since 1854, beginning with the first building of the Manhattan Gas Light Company at 4 Irving Place. In 1884, after the merger of several enterprises, the Consolidated Gas Company moved into the building, and within 15 years was the major supplier of gas to the city. By the early 1900s Consolidated Gas acquired several electric light firms such as the Edison Electric Illuminating Company, which opened its first power station on Pearl Street in 1882. The Consolidated Edison name was adopted in 1936. The company is now known as Con Edison.

Headquarters of Consolidated Gas Company on the southeast corner of Irving Place and East 15th Street. Construction of the new headquarters, seen at the rear, began in 1910. At the right, the Academy of Music

Academy of Music, just before demolition, 1926. When abandoned by the elite, the former opera house struggled along presenting popular entertainment, and then movies, for a mass audience.

GP15a The Con Edison offices are on the site of the **Academy of Music** (Alexander Saeltzer, 1854), a grand opera house built for New York's oldest and wealthiest families. This bastion of aristocratic New York society was celebrated in two of Edith Wharton's New York novels, *The Age of Innocence* and *The Custom of the Country*. Along with the opera, the Academy was the scene of many social events, including an historic reception for the Prince of Wales in 1860. Although the opera house seated 4,000, the coveted upper boxes were available on certain nights only to members of the aristocratic families. That exclusivity brought down the curtain on the Academy. The nouveaux riches triumphed with the opening of the Metropolitan Opera House on Broadway and West 39th Street in 1883 and patrons flocked uptown.

Cross Irving Place and East 17th street. Walk a few steps up Irving Place.

GP16 Two Greek Revival row houses (1840-1841) on the east side of Irving Place at Nos. 54 and 56 have been transformed into the **Inn at Irving Place** (renovations, Larry Wente of Gertier & Wente, 1991-1995). Each of the 12 rooms in the intimate European-style hotel is individually furnished and named for such neighborhood notables as Edith Wharton, O. Henry, Washington Irving, and Antonín Dvořák (from 1892-1895 the composer lived at 327 East 17th Street [demolished 1991], where he wrote his New World Symphony). Afternoon tea is served in the Lady Mendl parlor.

Continue walking up Irving Place to the southeast corner of East 18th Street.

GP17 **Pete's Tavern**, 66 Irving Place, is one of the oldest surviving drinking establishments in the city. As early as 1852 a "grocery" (sometimes a euphemism for a tavern in that era) operated in this building. The first official saloon here opened in 1892, and seven years later Thomas and John Healy leased the premises and named it Healy's Tavern.

O. Henry was a regular at Healy's, where he mingled with coach drivers and other working men, picking up dialects, characters, and ideas for his stories. His pungent short story "The Lost Blend" is set in Healy's Tavern (disguised as "Kenealy's"). A plaque over the second booth on the right inside Pete's asserts that O. Henry wrote his

Healy's Tavern (later Pete's Tavern), 1909. A Star of David appears on the sign advertising Ehret's Beer.

poignant Christmas story "The Gift of the Magi" at that spot. Although this is challenged by the plaque at No. 55, both claims have merit. According to accounts of people who were with the author, O. Henry hatched the plot at Healy's but returned to his lodgings at No. 55 to write the story.

Cross East 18th Street. Turn right and walk to the first group of row houses on the north side of the street.

GP18 An elegant row of five Anglo-Italianate houses stretches from **Nos. 135-143** (1855). Beautifully preserved and remarkably intact, they evoke the character of the mid-19th-century neighborhood which surrounded Gramercy Park.

Return to Irving Place.

Pete's Tavern received its present name some time after 1928, when Peter D. Belles acquired the property. Drop in to see the ornate rosewood bar, pressed-metal ceilings, and tiled floors, and to enjoy the ambiance of an old-fashioned New York saloon.

Continue walking up Irving Place. Stop at East 19th Street

GP19 a-j East 19th St. between Irving Place and Third Avenue is known as **"The Block Beautiful,"** but could more aptly be called "The Block Bountiful." The delight here is found in the variety and abundance of remodeled row houses and stables peacefully co-existing on this quiet tree-lined street. The tone was set in the early 1900s when architect Frederick Sterner bought a brick house further down the block, reinvented it in a Mediterranean style, and then went on to redo several other houses on the block.

Begin to stroll down the block.

Notable is the tiny, Dutch-gabled structure at No. 124 and the elaborate former carriage house at No. 129 with its diamond-paned leaded-glass windows and neo-Gothic trim. The unusual stuccoed apartment house at No. 132 was designed by Sterner in 1911. No. 135 with its brick and stone Tudor-style facade, Gothic-style arched doorway, and small-paned windows, remodeled by Sterner in the 1920s for a banker, is now owned by designer Oleg Cassini. No. 139, Sterner's own stuccoed house, with its decorative tilework around the doorway, tiled planters, ornamental metalwork and tiled roof, stands in excellent condition. Nearby are two more stuccoed Sterners. No. 141, with its pair of jockeys on

North side of the "Block Beautiful," looking east in the early 1900s. At the left , two former stables, 127 and 129 East 19th Street.

pedestals belonged to a sportscaster. No. 145 is ornamented with graceful plaques. No. 143 is a contrarian on the block. It is a three-story Greek Revival row house with a brownstone basement and stoop, not remodeled, but restored to its original design. Two smaller Greek Revival dwellings stand at Nos. 144 and 146. Note the plaque on No. 146 where artist George Bellows added a top-floor studio to the house in which he lived and worked from 1910 to 1925.

GP20 Visible through the iron fence in the southeast corner of the park is **Fantasy Fountain** (Gregg Wyatt, 1983), a delightful sculptural grouping where dancing giraffes cavort under the smiling faces of the Moon God and Sun Goddess.

Retrace your steps to Irving Place and continue walking north. Cross Gramercy Park South to the park. Turn right and walk almost to the corner.

Walk to the corner.

GP21 Across Gramercy Park South at No. 28 stands the **Brotherhood Synagogue,** originally the Friends Meeting House (King & Kellum, 1857-1859). A triangular pediment crowns the beautifully proportioned structure whose austere Italianate design reflects the Quaker belief in simplicity. The Meeting House served as a station in the pre-Civil War Underground Railroad. In 1958, after the Society of Friends moved to Stuyvesant Square, the building was designated a landmark to protect it from demolition. Later acquired by the United Federation of Teachers, which planned to use it for offices and meeting space, it was sold to the Brotherhood Synagogue in 1974.

The congregation, affiliated with the Conservative branch of Judaism, was founded by Rabbi Irving J. Block in 1954 and shared space with the Village Presbyterian Church on West 13th Street before moving to Gramercy Park. Extensive structural repair and renovations were carried out on the building under the direction of architect James Stewart Polshek. Both Polshek and the project's contractor worked without a fee. In 1982 Polshek, Dean of Columbia University's School of Architecture, designed the adjoining **Garden of Remembrance**, a memorial to past members of the congregation and to the six million Jews who perished in the Holocaust.

Cross Gramercy Park South.

Just to the left of the synagogue is the Garden, a serene courtyard planted with honey locust trees facing the limestone memorial wall.

Return to the northwest corner of Gramercy Park South and the park.

GP22 The Gramercy (George Da Cunha, 1883), at No. 34, rises nine stories directly across from the park. It is the oldest surviving co-op in the city. As new construction continued to move further north in the late 19th century and the cost of individual houses soared, apartment house living gradually became an acceptable lifestyle for the wealthy. Co-ops were especially favored because of their exclusivity. Over the years film stars John Carradine, James Cagney, and Margaret Hamilton have lived here. The luxury Gramercy was built with hydraulic Otis elevators. When they were replaced by an electrical system in 1994, they were the oldest surviving in the city. The brick and brownstone facade of the Queen Anne building is enhanced by terra-cotta ornament. Cross over and look into the outer lobby to see the stained-glass ceiling and tiled floor.

GP23 Next door at **No. 36**, two silver-painted plaster knights guard the entrance to another co-op apartment house (James Riely Gordon, 1908-10). Built in a U-shape, its two towers rise 12 stories and are topped by a

The Gramercy co-op looking east from Gramercy Park, c. 1890.

recessed penthouse. The building is clad in glazed white terra cotta above a granite basement and designed with elaborate neo-Gothic detailing. Note the first- and second-story windows linked by a lively tracery design and topped with a graceful ogee arch. Beginning at the fourth story, projecting oriels decorated with crowned shields supported by cherubs continue to the height of the building; gargoyles spring from the tenth-story cornice. Actor John Barrymore and sculptor Daniel Chester French were residents in this medieval fantasy overlooking the park.

GP24 In the mid-19th century two leaders of American industry, Peter Cooper and Cyrus Field, lived next to

Walk to Gramercy Park North. Turn left and walk to Lexington Avenue. Cross Gramercy Park North to the northeast corner.

each other on the east side of Lexington Avenue in the block between East 21st and East 22nd Streets (plaques mark both locations). Field's opulently decorated mansion stood at **123 East 21st Street**. Field formed a company with Cooper and Samuel F. B. Morse that laid the Atlantic Cable in 1858. Morse, a prominent artist who invented the electric telegraph system and the Morse code, lived nearby on West 22nd Street.

Walk up Lexington Avenue to the southeast corner of East 22nd Street.

Gramercy Park North, east of Lexington Avenue, 1905. At far left, the former Cyrus Field mansion renovated in 1901 by Stanford White for Henry W. Poor.

GP25 On the southeast corner of East 22nd Street at **9 Lexington Avenue** stood the simply furnished red-brick house of inventor-entrepreneur Peter Cooper. A self-made millionaire, Cooper amassed a fortune in enterprises as varied as the manufacture of glue and telegraph wires. His ironworks produced structural building beams and America's first steam locomotive, the "Tom Thumb." He was a noted civic leader and philanthropist who in 1859 established the still-thriving Cooper Union for the Advancement of Science and Art, a private, tuition-free college on Astor Place. After Cooper's death in 1883, his daughter Sarah Amelia, her husband Abram S. Hewitt (mayor of New York, 1887-1888), and their children moved into the 25-room home.

Peter Cooper house just before demolition, 1940. Stanford White added the portico and redecorated the interior for the Hewitt family. Mayor's lamps flank the entrance.

GP26 Three distinctive buildings stand on the other corners of Lexington Avenue and East 22nd Street. On the southwest corner at No. 4 is **The Sage House,** now apartments, originally the Russell Sage Foundation (Grosvenor Atterbury, 1912-1915; addition, 1929-1931). It was built for the charitable organization founded by philanthropist Olivia Sage in 1907 and named for her late husband. At age 77 Mrs. Sage inherited $65 million accumulated by her tight-fisted financier spouse and spent the rest of her life (she died at 90) giving generously to advance the cause of social reform. The building, acquired by the Roman Catholic Archdiocese of New York in 1949, was used as the Catholic Charities Building until 1974. The rough-cut sandstone building is designed in the form of a Florentine palazzo. Panels carved by René Chambellan symbolizing education, civics, health, and other concerns of the foundation adorn the facade. A frieze over the ornate iron door of the original main entrance at 130 East 22nd Street depicts the Trees of Life and Knowledge.

GP27 Occupying the northwest corner of East 22nd Street is **The New Manhattan High School Collaborative,** originally the Manhattan Trade School for Girls (C.B.J.

Snyder, 1915-1919). The white terra-cotta-clad, exterior with Gothic detailing stands in contrast to the loft-like interior designed for instruction in the garment trades. Look for small figures holding books and tools just below the cornice. The School of the Future, part of the city's new Collaborative High School program, is housed in the building.

Turn right on East 22nd Street and walk a few steps.

GP28 You are entering the south campus of **Baruch College,** an independent senior college of the City University of New York (CUNY). Two former courthouses of the Domestic Relations Court, both currently part of Baruch College, stand side by side on the north side of East 22nd Street just east of Lexington Avenue. The ten-story Art Deco corner building at No. 135, now the **Administrative Building** of Baruch College, was the Family Court Building (Charles B. Meyers, 1938-1940). Aluminum relief panels (designed by H.P. Camden) illustrate family life, extolling such virtues as work, prayer and, study. Over the main doorway, between figures of Justice and Liberty, an eagle perches on the seal of the Domestic Relations Court. Changing exhibitions of art and photography at the Sidney Mishkin Gallery are open to the public, Monday through Friday from noon to 5:00 P.M.

GP29 The building next door at No. 137, Baruch's **School of Public Affairs,** was the Children's Court Building, (Crow, Lewis & Wickenhoefer, 1912-1916). It was designed in the Italian Renaissance style with a row of six two-story Ionic columns above a rusticated base. After a new Family Courthouse opened on Foley Square in the mid-1970s, the city transferred ownership of these courthouses to Baruch College.

Return to Lexington Avenue and continue walking to East 23rd Street.

GP30 The 16-story, tan-brick and limestone building at 17 Lexington Avenue is **Baruch College,** formerly the College of the City of New York (Thompson, Holmes & Converse, 1928). It replaces the Free Academy, a high school for boys founded in 1849, designed in the Gothic Revival style by noted architect James Renwick Jr. In

The College of the
City of New York in
1912.

1866 the Free Academy became the College of the City
of New York, popularly known as City College or CCNY.
When City College moved to its new campus uptown in
Hamilton Heights in 1907, the business departments
remained behind. In 1919 the School of Business and
Civic Administration was founded. In 1953 it became
formally known as the Bernard M. Baruch School of Business and Public Administration, named in honor of
economist and financier Bernard Baruch, Class of 1889, a
trusted economic advisor to six U.S. presidents from
Wilson to Truman. By 1968 Baruch College emerged as a
separate senior college, part of the CUNY system. The
college enrolls over 15,000 students and enjoys a
national reputation for excellence in business education
and public administration.

GP31 The 20-story **Kenmore Hotel** (Maurice Deutsch,
1927-1928) at 145 East 23rd Street stands on the site of
a building at Nos. 143-147 that housed the Art Students
League on three floors from 1887 until 1892. The
League was founded in 1875 by a group of students
from the National Academy of Design which stood on

Turn right on East
23rd Street. Walk
to the bus shelter
and look across
the street.

the northwest corner of Fourth Avenue and East 23rd
Street from 1865 to 1899. Over 600 students attended
classes at the League taught by such notables as William
Merritt Chase, Kenyon Cox, Augustus Saint-Gaudens,
and Thomas Eakins.

After the League moved to its present home on West
57th Street in 1892, the building filled with impover-
ished artists and others living in a warren of tiny ateliers.
Stephen Crane lived here on and off for two years (1893-
1895), eking out a marginal living writing short pieces
and stories of city life for newspapers and magazines.
Crane worked in his cramped, dark studio room on his
classic Civil War novel *The Red Badge of Courage*, which first
appeared in serial form in a Philadelphia newspaper in
1895.

The Kenmore Hotel is currently under renovation,
managed by the not-for-profit Housing and Services
agency. The hotel has seen better days. Nathanael West,
author of *Miss Lonlyhearts* and *The Day of the Locust*, worked
here as night manager from 1927 to 1929, using the late
evening hours to write. West held a perpetual open-
house for his freeloading literary friends including his
brother-in-law, humorist S.J. Perelman, journalist
Quentin Reynolds, critic Edmund Wilson, and authors
Erskine Caldwell and James T. Farrell, providing them
with free rooms, meals, and the use of the swimming
pool. Dashiell Hammett, about to be evicted from
another hotel for non-payment, came to the Kenmore to
finish *The Maltese Falcon*.

Return to Lexing-
ton Avenue. Cross
Lexington Avenue
and East 23rd
Street to the north-
west corner.

GP32 The **George Washington Hotel** (Frank M.
Andrews, 1928) stands on the northeast corner of Lexington Avenue. In 1939 writers W.H. Auden and
Christopher Isherwood arrived from England and
checked into the hotel. Isherwood soon left for Califor-
nia, but Auden remained in what he later described as
"much the nicest hotel in town." After a two-month stay
Auden, one of the major English poets of the century,
penned a five-page poem of thanks to the manager on
hotel stationery. The poem is now in the Berg Collection
of rare manuscripts in the New York Public Library.

GP33 The modest four-story brick houses at **132 and 134 East 24th Street** fit the description of the house (no longer standing) at 104 East 26th Street where author Herman Melville lived for the last 28 years of his life. The author's granddaughter describes the Melvilles' muddy-yellow brick house with its brownstone trim "looking like every other house in the row." That row on East 26th Street is gone, but these look-alikes survive. (More on Herman Melville at the end of this tour.)

Continue walking north on Lexington Avenue. Cross East 24th Street. Turn left and walk a few steps.

GP34 The buff-colored brick building on the southwest corner at 130 East 25th Street is currently the **Friends House in Rosehill** (renovations, Harden Van Arnam, 1995-1996), a Quaker-sponsored residence for people living with AIDS. Rosehill, a term still used to define this neighborhood, was the name of the summer mansion of Tory sympathizer John Watts, who purchased Stuyvesant farmland stretching from the present East 21st to East 30th Street, Broadway to the East River. The seven-story building with adjoining four-story annex to the west was originally the B.W. Mayer Building (Herman Lee Meader, 1915-1916), constructed with stores on the ground floor, offices and showrooms above.

Return to the corner. Walk up Lexington Avenue. Cross East 25th Street to the northwest corner.

It was purchased by the International Ladies Garment Workers Union in 1923 for offices, and acquired in 1930 by Local 3 of the International Brotherhood of Electrical Workers for its headquarters and trade school. In 1971 the first accredited Labor College in the nation was established here as a division of Empire State College, the State University of New York. The Society of Friends bought the building in 1994 and converted it into a facility with 50 efficiency apartments, a dining room, community rooms, recreational area, and a library. A rooftop garden is also proposed. The Friends provide meals, counseling, clinical supervision, and healthcare to residents.

Note the striking terra-cotta ornament of coiled snakes and cattle skulls above the second story, and the Mayan-style head guarding the entrance. Several other buildings by the architect, Herman Lee Meader, display fanciful ornament (manufactured by the New York

Cross Lexington Avenue. Walk east on East 25th Street to the middle of the block.

Architectural Terra Cotta Company), most notably his Cliff Dwellers' Apartments (1914) at Riverside Drive and 96th Street.

GP35 The new **Academic Complex of Baruch College** (Kohn Pederson Fox Associates, 1997-2001, expected completion date) will fill almost the whole block from Lexington Avenue to just before Third Avenue between East 24th and East 25th Streets. The 200-foot structure will feature a ten-story atrium clad in silver aluminum rising from a reddish-brick base designed to relate to Baruch's library opposite on East 25th Street.

Computer simulation of the Academic Complex of Baruch College, scheduled to open in the year 2001.

The $250 million building will house research facilities, classrooms, and faculty offices. It will also include a physical fitness center with gym and swimming pool, a theater and recital space, and a television studio.

GP35a A string of four horse-related buildings once owned by the **Fiss, Doerr, and Carroll Horse Company** formerly occupied most of this block. A seven-story,

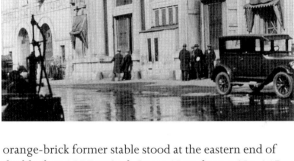

Buildings owned by Fiss, Doerr, and Carroll Horse Company were demolished in 1997 for the new Baruch College Academic Complex. At right 147 East 24th Street, with a soaring arched-steel supporting roof built to cover a huge horse rink and spectator's gallery. On the left, is one of the stables on the block.

orange-brick former stable stood at the eastern end of the block at 155 East 24th Street. Next door at No. 147 was a Beaux-Arts barrel-vaulted horse auction mart. Both were designed by Horgan and Slattery in 1907. Six years later the same architects built another stable at No. 139. Also demolished for the Academic Center was an 1880s stable at No. 145 and two small, deteriorating hotels on Lexington Avenue, the Hotel Amsterdam on the southeast corner of East 25th Street and the Hotel Gramercy on the northeast corner of East 24th Street.

GP36 The massive Romanesque Revival building at 151 East 25th Street extending to East 26th Street was originally the Lexington Building (G.B. Waite, 1895). Now the **William and Anita Newman Library of Baruch College**

If possible, cross to the south side of East 25th Street. (for the next few years construction may make this difficult.)

(renovations, Davis Brody & Associates, 1992-1994), the seven-story structure is faced with Pompeian brick and trimmed in terra cotta with a base of red Maine granite. It was built to be a power station for the Lexington Avenue cable system of the Metropolitan Street Railway Company. The Lexington line, one of several cable railways in the city, ran four miles from East 23rd to East 105th Street and was the last cable street railway installed in the nation. By the turn of the century electric streetcars (commonly called trolleys) began to replace cable cars. The 20-foot high arches running along East 25th Street, now windows and a doorway, were built as entrances for cable cars into the building. Cable machinery and engines were housed in the lower stories of the East 25th Street portion of the enormous powerhouse, while boilers and coal storage vaults were in the rear, with warehouse and factory space above. In recent years the building has been occupied by printing companies, garment factories, a carpentry school, and a garage.

Now a high-tech library and technology center, this stunning example of adaptive use received the New York Landmarks Conservancy Lucy G. Moses Preservation Award in 1994. It contains more than 270,000 volumes, 2,000 current periodicals, a large microform collection, audiovisual materials and multimedia CD-ROM, and banks of computer workstations. Step inside to view the handsome interior with its soaring, glass-topped atrium.

Return to Lexington Avenue. Stop at the northeast corner of East 25th Street.

GP37 The brick fortress on the west side of Lexington Avenue between East 25th and East 26th Streets is the **69th Regiment Armory** (Joseph Howland Hunt and Richard Howland Hunt, 1904-1906). It was built for the "Fighting 69th" of the 165th Infantry, a famed regiment of New York Irishmen founded in 1851. The brigade served with distinction in every major campaign from Bull Run to Appomattox during the Civil War, and fought in the Spanish-American War and the Mexican border wars. During World War I, legendary heroes Colonel William "Wild Bill" Donovan, chaplain Father Francis P. Duffy, and poet Joyce Kilmer were with the 69th in bitter fighting in France. The combat unit last

fought in campaigns in the Pacific during World War II.
It later became a unit of the New York Army National
Guard's 42nd (Rainbow) Division.

Armories began to appear in New York City in the
mid-19th century as headquarters for local militia, their
impenetrable castle-like exteriors symbolizing the rule of
law and order. Here the architects broke with that
medieval tradition and designed a building with over-
scaled Beaux-Arts detailing topped by a mansard roof.
The interior houses administrative quarters as well as a
vast drill hall suitable for athletic events and art exhibitions.

This was the site of the 1913 Armory Show that
shocked the American art world. Officially the International Exhibition of Modern Art, the controversial show
displayed works of contemporary American artists along
with the European avant-garde. The work of noncon-
formist American painters was overshadowed by the rad-
icalism of European modernists: Impressionist, Post-
Impressionist, Fauvist, and Cubist painters and sculptors,
many exhibiting for the first time in the United States.
Among the artists with work on view were Picasso,
Cézanne, Braque, Gauguin, Van Gogh, and Matisse. The
reaction of visitors and press to the month-long show
(February 17th to March 15th) was overwhelmingly
negative. Marcel Duchamp's *Nude Descending a Staircase* was
met with ridicule. Theodore Roosevelt called the artists
"a bunch of lunatics." While the general public was out-
raged, private collectors began to acquire the avant-garde
artwork. The Armory Show challenged American artists
to move toward modernism and marked the end of the
domination of the art world by traditionalists.

Just to the right of the entrance is a plaque commem-
orating the Armory Show.

GP38 It's easy to miss the tiny plaque on the side of the
delivery entrance to 357 Park Avenue South. The plaque
marks the site of the house at **104 East 26th Street** where
author Herman Melville lived with his family from 1863
to 1891. Melville was born in 1819 at 6 Pearl Street in
lower Manhattan to a prominent family that soon fell on

Cross Lexington
Avenue at East
25th Street.

Walk to East 26th
Street. Turn left
and continue
walking just past
the rear of the
armory.

hard times. As a young man he shipped out to sea in a series of voyages that became the inspiration for much of his literary work. The vagabond sailor-author became well-known as a young man who had mutinied, jumped ship, been captured by cannibals, and lived to write popular adventure books about it all. In 1851 his popularity plunged when readers couldn't fathom *Moby Dick*, the story of life on a whaling ship in an ocean of symbolism.

In 1863 Melville, with his wife Elizabeth and their children, moved into a small, brick row house at 60 East 26th Street (renumbered 104 East 26th Street in 1868) where he lived in obscurity for the rest of his life. For almost 20 years (1866-1885) the author toiled in a low-paying job as an inspector in the U.S. Customs Service on the Gansevoort Docks of the Hudson River while continuing to write. *Billy Budd,* completed during the final year of his life, was packed in a trunk after his death and was not published until 1924, when scholars and critics began to recognize Melville's literary genius. Some three decades earlier his 1891 obituary in *The World* had read, "Herman Melville, formerly a well-known author...."

Continue a few steps to the west where a variety of restaurants and cafes are to be found on Park Avenue South.

Herman Melville, c. 1861. Shunned by critics and readers, he faced literary oblivion.

Looking west down 23rd Street from Fifth Avenue in the 1890s. At right is the Fifth Avenue Hotel.

Ladies' Mile Walk

Introduction:

Shopping as a national pastime had its origins in the years following the Civil War in an area called Ladies' Mile, originally identifying the stretch of Broadway from East 10th Street to Madison Square. The name was later used to describe the larger shopping district that developed from a few blocks below Union Square to Madison Square along Broadway, Sixth Avenue, and West 23rd Street. As commerce moved north, residents fled uptown leaving their fashionable dwellings to be converted to stores or demolished to make way for enormous, ornate emporiums. Small shops, restaurants, cafes, and confectioners lined once-quiet avenues transformed into bustling thoroughfares crowded with carriages and streetcars. Beginning in 1878 the elevated railroad along Sixth Avenue brought thousands of riders daily for the thrilling adventure of shopping in a variety of magnificent department stores. The splendid commercial palaces, French Second Empire, Beaux-Arts and Renaissance-style structures of Stern Brothers, Lord & Taylor, Siegel-Cooper, Arnold Constable, and other leading merchants catered to every taste. Architecture and merchandising had come together to create a dazzling setting for consumerism.

Until the mid-19th century, shoppers in the city patronized tiny specialty shops in lower Manhattan like Samuel Lord's store, which opened on Catherine Street in 1826 and sold dry goods. (The term "dry goods" originated with New England merchants whose main imports were bolts of cloth and rum, the latter referred to as "wet goods".) The modern American department store was born in 1846 when merchandising genius A.T. Stewart opened his marble palace at Broadway and Reade Street (Joseph Trench & Co., extant). Although limited to fabrics, women's clothing, and accessories, ladies now could shop on different specialty floors under the same roof rather than traveling to numerous shops for their

R. H. Macy's first store, on the west side of Sixth Avenue just above West 14th Street, c. 1858.

purchases. Catering to women only, the emerging department store helped to establish the practice of set prices and introduced the first fashion shows to America.

Stewart's next enterprise opened on Broadway between East 9th and East 10th Streets as a full-fledged department store (John Kellum, 1862; demolished, 1956). Shoppers could find at the A.T. Stewart store a seemingly endless variety of merchandise: clothing for women, men, and children, fine fabrics, household furnishings, and imported carpets displayed in separate departments. Compulsive shopper Mary Todd Lincoln redecorated the White House with goods purchased primarily from the A.T. Stewart store. The spectacular five-story cast-iron building in the form of a Renaissance palazzo, with its central rotunda and glass skylight, set the standard for department store design and heralded the birth of Ladies' Mile on Broadway.

By 1868 Arnold Constable (which had made several earlier moves) arrived on Broadway and East 19th Street where it set up shop specializing in fine clothing in a huge, marble-faced emporium with Renaissance-inspired ornament. One block north in 1870 Lord & Taylor (also continuing its uptown migration) began catering to the fashionable in a splendid French Second Empire, iron-fronted building. W. & J. Sloane sold carpeting and Oriental rugs in its massive 1882 stone and brick structure while across Broadway in a Queen Anne brick building, the Gorham Company offered silver, glassware, and other luxury items.

Sixth Avenue became another major shopping street. By the 1840s it had been built up as a fashionable residential neighborhood with brick- and stone-fronted houses above 14th Street. In 1858 former sea captain Rowland Hussey Macy opened a small dry goods store in a row house on the west side of Sixth Avenue just above West 14th Street and rapidly expanded into the neighboring houses. Hugh O'Neill and Adams Dry Goods both began in former dwellings which were later demolished for the construction of their grand department stores.

A number of the leading emporiums, notably B. Altman and Stern Brothers, were iron-fronted buildings. Although constructed in stages, often years apart, duplicate iron castings were used to form unified facades. Cast-iron technology was well-suited to the construction of department stores. Since cast-iron columns could bear tremendous weight, they were placed far apart, opening up interior space for display and creating large expanses on the exterior for glass show windows. The new technology provided an opportunity for respectable women to walk unescorted on the streets as "window shopping" emerged as a novel diversion for Victorian ladies.

Ladies' Mile flourished until World War I when retailers, following their wealthy clientele north, moved the city's major shopping district to an area between 34th and 59th Streets centered on Fifth Avenue. Over the years the once-elegant department stores deteriorated as the abandoned structures were converted to lofts for storage, wholesalers, and light manufacturing. In the 1970s the neighborhood began to diversify as photographers, design studios, advertising agencies, publishers, and architectural firms moved into the derelict buildings, attracted by low rents and large spaces.

Galvanized by preservationists who organized a major campaign to protect the great buildings, the New York City Landmarks Preservation Commission designated the **Ladies' Mile Historic District** in 1989, sparking a commercial renaissance. The landmark district extends from portions of West 15th Street to West 24th Street between Broadway and Sixth Avenue, at some points reaching to mid-block between Sixth and Seventh Avenues on the west and just short of Park Avenue South on the east. Today business is thriving, national retailers occupy many of the restored buildings, small stores line the streets, and shoppers once again crowd the sidewalks.

Tour

The tour begins on the north side of West 23rd Street several steps west of Fifth Avenue. Look across at the row of small-scale buildings on the south side of the street.

(Buildings visible to the east from this point are described in the **Madison Square Tour.**)

West 23rd Street between Fifth and Sixth Avenues was a fashionable residential block of 1850s brownstone row houses before it evolved into a major artery of the Ladies' Mile. The character of the neighborhood began to change in the 1870s as private dwellings were converted for business use. A few of the original structures survive with some of the upper stories still intact. Others are completely hidden behind commercial facades. The 1854 Italianate row house at **No. 20** retains its original window enframements on the top three stories as well as its metal-bracketed cornice. It stands as a reminder of the homes that once lined this block.

LM1 No trace of the original facade remains at **No. 14**, the Anglo-Italianate brownstone residence where Edith Newbold Jones, better known as Edith Wharton, was born on January 24, 1862. Although the Jones family lived in Europe for long periods of time, Edith's impres-

West 23rd Street looking west from Fifth Avenue, 1884. The first row house is No. 14, birthplace of Edith Wharton, with the top stories intact and the bottom altered for commercial use.

sionable teen years were spent here in the affluent neighborhood of Madison Square. The aristocratic Jones family belonged to the elite New York society that Wharton brilliantly portrays in her great novels *The Age of Innocence*, *The Custom of the Country* and *The House of Mirth*. She wrote more than forty books, including the classic *Ethan Frome*, and was the first woman to receive the Pulitzer Prize. Recognized as one of America's greatest authors, she lived in Europe after 1913 and died in France in 1937.

Edith Jones in Newport, Rhode Island in 1884. The following year she married Edward Wharton.

Although Edith Wharton's birthplace still stands, it has been completely altered. The house was converted for "gentlemen's apartments" above and stores below (Henry J. Hardenbergh, 1882). Ten years later it was renovated and given a cast-iron front (George H. Budlong, 1892); later the building was altered again (Henry C. Pelton, 1907) for the linen store of James McCutcheon & Company.

Edith Jones married Edward "Teddy" Wharton on April 29, 1885, in a subdued ceremony in Trinity Chapel (Richard Upjohn,

Edith Wharton fans should detour to West 25th Street west of Broadway and then return to West 23rd Street.

1850-1855), the austere brownstone church on the north side of West 25th Street. The wedding breakfast was held afterward in her mother's house (no longer standing) across the street at 28 West 25th Street. The marriage was not a happy one and the couple divorced in 1913. Both this church and the 1846 Trinity Church downtown were designed by renowned ecclesiastical architect Richard Upjohn in the Gothic Revival style. In the 1940s the Episcopal church was converted to the Serbian Orthodox Cathedral of St. Sava and is open to the public during Sunday morning services.

Continue walking west on West 23rd Street to the parking lot just past No. 37.

LM2 The dazzling white iron-fronted structure on the south side of West 23rd Street at Nos. 32-46 is the former **Stern Brothers** (Henry Fernbach, Hugo Kafka, William Schickel & Co., built in five stages from 1878-1892). One of the greatest department stores on Ladies' Mile, Stern Brothers, operated by four brothers and three sisters, was known for high-quality merchandise as well as attentive service to the affluent customers who arrived at this splendid establishment in their private carriages.

West 23rd Street looking west in 1878. The large building is the new Stern Brothers, whose construction hastened the demise of the residential neighborhood.

The building is in the commercial palace style. It recalls the massing and ornament of an Italian Renaissance palazzo, but with rows of large glass windows to bring needed light to the interior, and sizable show windows on the ground floor to lure people inside to shop. Stern Brothers extends to West 22nd Street with a rear facade of brick above a cast-iron base. The present building is a skillful enlargement (William Schickel, 1892) of the original structure, which was the eastern wing (a story has been added and its entrance removed). The earlier design was repeated in the west wing by using duplicate iron castings of the original. The new central section unites both wings in a projecting pavilion with a splendid arched entrance. Note the fine Renaissance detailing and the monogram "SB" in the cartouche above the lion's head over the arch.

West 23rd Street looking east to Fifth Avenue with the Flatiron Building, c. 1903. In the center, the expanded Stern Brothers. Signs on the right identify Teller & Company (Later Bonwit Teller) and Best & Company.

LM3 and 4 To the west of Stern Brothers stood other prominent New York retailers, **Teller & Company** (later Bonwit Teller) at No. 58 (from 1895-1911) and **Best & Company** at Nos. 60-62 (from 1881-1910).

LM5 Turn around and look north through the parking lot to the top stories of a small peaked-roof building at **22 West 24th Street.** This was Stanford White's luxuriously furnished hideaway. A red velvet swing and a curtained canopy bed with mirrors and tiny twinkling colored lights took center stage in the architect's design for pleasure. It was here in 1901 that White's affair with showgirl Evelyn Nesbit was initiated, a liaison that led to his murder five years later by her deranged husband, Harry K. Thaw.

Continue walking. Stop just before the corner of Sixth Avenue.

LM6 The parking lot on the southeast corner of Sixth Avenue marks the site of the spectacular **Booth Theatre** (Renwick & Sands, 1868-1869). Founded by actor Edwin Booth, the theater was designed in the French Second Empire style and held an audience of 1,800. It was a marvel of advanced design and technology and featured an enormous stage, an innovative sunken orchestra pit, and hydraulic machinery for changing scenery. Booth was a better actor than businessman and the theater was a

The Booth Theatre, c. 1870. Horse-drawn trolleys ran along Sixth Avenue before the construction of the elevated railway in 1878.

Cross West 23rd Street and walk back to the former Stern Brothers.

Turn to view the north side of West 23rd Street.

financial failure. It was remodeled by McCreery's Department Store in the mid-1880s and stood until 1975. Construction of a residential building is planned for the site. (More on Booth in the **Gramercy Park** tour.)

Corporate offices of Bozel Worldwide and the Toy Division of Hasbro Industries currently occupy the meticulously restored Stern building. Note the delicate castings of ivy-twined colonettes on the facade and the replica gas lamps lining the bluestone sidewalk.

LM7 By the 1880s this block of West 23rd Street was one long mall, offering consumers a tantalizing array of merchandise and services. The imposing six-story red-brick building trimmed with brownstone (William Schickel, 1880-1881) in the middle of the block at **Nos. 27-33** was home to E.P. Dutton Publishers and the Knickerbocker Press of G.P. Putnam & Sons. The building also housed silk, underwear, and upholstery merchants.

LM8 To the west is a five-story brick building at **Nos. 35-37** (D. & J. Jardine, 1879-1880). It originally belonged to D.S. Hess, a furniture and home decoration company. Subsequent tenants have included Villeroy and Boch, specializing in china and glass, and F.A.O. Schwarz toys, which later moved next door to Nos. 39-41. An unusual galvanized iron cornice with ornaments of acanthus leaves and sunflowers tops the building.

LM9 The dignified, eight-story limestone structure at **Nos. 43-47** (Henry J. Hardenbergh, 1893-1894) was influenced by Renaissance designs. It was built for offices and retail stores offering such merchandise as china, glassware, and furniture. Now the Castro Building, it is a showroom and clearance center for the convertible sofa manufacturer.

F.A.O. Schwarz Toy Store at 39-41 West 23rd Street, 1899.

Walk west toward Sixth Avenue.

Eden Musee in 1891. Modeled after Madame Tussaud's wax museum in London, it stood at 55 West 23rd Street from 1884 to 1915. Kinetoscopic peep shows and early silent films were shown in the theater cafe on the ground floor.

LM10 Near the end of the block at **Nos. 61-65** (John B. Snook, 1886, additions 1894) is the seven-story cast-iron commercial palace that once housed Horner's Furniture Store (which became Flint and Horner) and later Villeroy and Boch. The large, square-headed windows brought natural light into the dimly lit showrooms.

81

LM11 The **Masonic Building** (Harry P. Knowles, 1911-1913), a 19-story, limestone and brick office and loft building, stands on the northeast corner of Sixth Avenue and West 23rd Street. A commercial enterprise, its income supports the charitable projects of the Grand Lodge of Free and Accepted Masons of the State of New York. The Freemasons, an international fraternal and philanthropic organization, evolved from stonemason guilds established in England and Scotland during the Middle Ages. The first

The present Masonic Building stands on the site of the first Masonic Hall, (Napoleon LeBrun, 1875), pictured here.

Masonic lodge in New York City was founded in 1739. Prominent members have included John Jacob Astor, Theodore Roosevelt, Fiorello H. LaGuardia, George M. Cohan, and Irving Berlin.

Directly in back of the building is Masonic Hall (Harry P. Knowles, 1905-1907). It holds the Grand Lodge Room, a splendid auditorium seating 1,200 people, and a dozen elaborately decorated two-story ceremonial Lodge Rooms ablaze with color and ornament. The ritual spaces were designed to evoke architectural eras ranging from Egyptian, Greek, Gothic, and Renaissance to the Colonial period. A ten-year, $15 million restoration of the building (Felix Chavez, Fine Art Decorating, 1986-1996) renewed the luster of the rooms. The Livingston Masonic Library is open to the public weekdays from 8:30 A.M. to 4:30 P.M. Free tours of the Lodge Rooms of Masonic Hall are available from 11:00 A.M. to 3:00 P.M. Enter through the lobby at 71 West 23rd Street.

Cross West 23rd Street to the northeast corner of Sixth Avenue.

In the late 19th century the area stretching from roughly West 23rd to West 30th Streets, west of Sixth Avenue was the center of a brassy amusement and vice district of dance halls, gambling dens, bordellos, saloons, and popular entertainment called **The Tenderloin**. The name was coined by Police Captain Alexander "Clubber" Williams, who boasted that he would be eating only tenderloin after his appointment to this precinct protected by Tammany Hall and police graft. Authors Stephen Crane and O. Henry, captured the raffish spirit of The Tenderloin in sketches and short stories.

LM12 The building that once housed **Koster & Bial's Music Hall**, a well-known vaudeville theater, stood on West 23rd Street just west of Sixth Avenue until 1924.

All that remains of the popular establishment is a forlorn structure at **729 Sixth Avenue** on the southwest corner of West 24th Street that held the German-style beer garden annex. Look for the inscription, "The Corner, Koster & Bial" in the pediment.

The opening of the elevated railway on Sixth Avenue in 1878 brought masses of middle-class customers to stores along the street. (The legend is that after the elevated tracks were demolished in 1939, the steel scrap was sold to Japan for their war industries.) Although Sixth Avenue was renamed Avenue of the Americas in 1945, New Yorkers have resisted the change and continue to call the street by its original name. Sixth Avenue and surrounding blocks from West 19th Street to West 26th Street have become the center of a thriving district of indoor and outdoor dealers selling affordable antiques and collectibles.

Koster & Bial's, 1892. In 1879 former brewers John Koster and Adam Bial turned Bryant's Opera House (1870) into a vaudeville theater. In 1895 they moved to West 34th Street where Macy's stands today.

Walk north along
Sixth Avenue to
West 24th Street.

LM13 On weekends thousands of people crowd into the
Annex Antique Fair and Flea Market, a neighborhood
tradition for over 20 years, located on a series of parking
lots along the east side of Sixth Avenue from West 24th
to West 26th Streets. The quintessential shopping adventure is to be found here as hundreds of vendors offer a
prodigious assortment of merchandise at bargain prices.
Current plans for construction of residential buildings on
several of the lots may force the markets to relocate.

Look up Sixth
Avenue.

Looking south down Sixth Avenue at the striking
panorama of glorious buildings, it is hard to imagine
their former state of decay. By the 1980s the once splendid department stores, neglected and underutilized for
more than 60 years, loomed over the avenue like a commercial ghost town. Recognized by concerned preservationists, rescued by the New York City Landmarks
Preservation Commission, and brought back to life by
building owners and major retailers, Sixth Avenue has
been revitalized as a leading shopping district in the city.

Retrace your steps
south on Sixth
Avenue. Cross
West 23rd Street
to the southeast
corner.

Look across Sixth
Avenue.

LM14 The former **Erich Brothers,** Nos. 695-709
(William Schickel, 1889; additions, Buchman & Deisler,
1894; further additions, Buchman & Fox, 1902), spans
most of the west side of the block from West 22nd Street
to West 23rd Street. Over the years, as business boomed,
the iron-fronted commercial palace was enlarged several
times. Each cast-iron addition replicated the original
Renaissance-style forms. When the building was
extended to the south in 1902 with a stuccoed brick
facade, that addition was designed and painted to copy
the original cast-iron building.

As the shopping district began moving north, the
Erichs retired and closed the store. Chicago retailer J.L.
Kesner leased the building and added new storefronts
with earth-toned tilework pilasters incorporating the letter "K," on the ground floor (Taylor & Levi, 1911). Over
the years the building was converted to lofts; it deteriorated until a recent renovation (Frank Richard Gen-
corelli, 1995). It is currently occupied by the Burlington
Coat Factory and the office supply company Staples.

LM15 On the corner of Sixth Avenue at **100 West 23rd Street** (Theodore Trebit, 1871) stands a classic "hold-out" building whose owner refused to sell to the Erich Brothers. The five-story, cast-iron corner building, with delightful iron cresting at the roofline, was constructed for a jewelry company. In 1897 William B. Riker opened a drugstore here, the first in a chain that later became Liggetts. The building is in disrepair and presents a sad contrast to its newly refurbished neighbor.

Walk south down Sixth Avenue. Stop mid-block between West 22nd and West 21st Streets.

LM16 The former **Adams Dry Goods Store,** Nos. 675-691 (DeLemos & Cordes, 1900-1902), is directly across Sixth Avenue. Samuel Adams opened his first dry goods store on the southwest corner of Sixth Avenue and West 22nd Street in 1885 in a brick dwelling altered for commercial use. Within four years his successful business had expanded to the entire block of neighboring houses along Sixth Avenue to West 21st Street. The ornate, Beaux-Arts buff-colored-brick Adams Dry Goods building was erected in stages, beginning in 1900, so as not to interfere with the flourishing business. It replaced all the small structures along this Sixth Avenue blockfront as well as those 200 feet to the west.

The architects, DeLemos & Cordes, had earlier designed the Siegel-Cooper store (coming up soon on this tour). The highly ornamented facade is graced by a helmeted female head encircled by a leafy garland above the central entranceway and lions' heads over the two other entrances. Medallions at the second story are inscribed "ADG" but the imposing limestone columns and terra-cotta ornament are concentrated above to catch

The west side of Sixth Avenue between West 20th and West 22nd Streets in 1909. At left, Hugh O'Neill & Co. To the right, Adams Dry Goods Store.

the eye of passengers on the elevated trains. The Adams store sold a wide assortment of clothing, accessories, and furniture. Adams did not follow the exodus of large department stores moving further uptown, but closed down by World War I. The building became an Army storage facility, a Hershey Chocolate factory, and was later used for offices, storage and manufacturing. Current tenants include a Barnes & Noble bookstore, Mattel Toys, and Wunderman Cato Johnson, a behavioral communications firm.

LM17 Diagonally across Sixth Avenue at Nos. 655-671, the former **Hugh O'Neill's** department store (Mortimer C. Merritt, 1887 and 1890; addition, 1895) fills the block from West 20th Street to West 21st Street. Henry and Hugh O'Neill were early retailers on Sixth Avenue above 14th Street. In 1870 the two brothers bought a pair of houses on this block for their growing dry goods business located at Broadway and East 20th Street. Although all the property on the block was acquired within ten years (when Henry retired), it was not until 1886, when various leases expired, that plans for construction of a department store could proceed. The building was constructed in two stages. The first section was erected in just six months, illustrating the speed and efficiency of pre-fabricated cast-iron construction.

Hugh O'Neill's offered bargain-priced merchandise for the mass market.

The vast dry goods emporium, painted bright yellow, was anchored at each corner by a round tower capped with a Byzantine-like dome. The domes are gone but the retailer's name remains in the pediment. O'Neill's was known for aggressive advertising and cut-rate sales aimed at its working-class customers. After Hugh O'Neill's death in 1902 the business struggled on, finally closing by World War I. The building, along with others on Sixth Avenue, was remodeled into lofts. Today the Elsevier Science Publishing

Company is an occupant, along with Goldman's Treasures, a china, silver, and glassware retailer.

Go back to West 22nd Street. Cross Sixth Avenue.

Note the original iron-framed storefronts of the old Adams Dry Goods building before you enter Barnes & Noble through the door nearest to West 22nd Street. Walk through the music department and turn left to see the skylight court, originally topped by a stained glass dome, which runs the height of the building. Inner courts were often constructed in 19th-century department stores to bring natural light deep inside the buildings. At the same time the court added an aura of splendor to the interior space, enhancing the shopping experience.

You may want to take a break and relax on one of the comfortable seats or linger for a snack in the upstairs cafe before continuing the tour. Restrooms are available in the rear of the store.

Exit the store. Cross West 21st Street and turn right.

LM18 Just down the block at 98-110 West 21st Street is the **Third Sephardic Burial Ground** (1829-1851) of Congregation Shearith Israel ("remnant of Israel"). At the time the Sephardic graveyard was established in the 1820s, this was a rural area. Within 20 years Sixth Avenue began to develop as a residential street built up with four- and five-story houses.

The first group of Jews in the city, numbering just 23, were the descendants of Jews expelled from Spain and Portugal in 1492 who had found refuge in Holland. They were among those who had settled in the Dutch colony of Brazil, and were returning to the Netherlands after the Portuguese recaptured Brazil in 1654. Their tiny boat was seized by a Spanish pirate vessel and later captured by a French ship that dropped them in New Amsterdam. At first the small group held religious services in a windmill; later, they worshiped in several locations downtown. By the time the congregation moved to their new Palladian-style synagogue (Robert Mook, 1859-1860) at 5 West 19th Street in a fashionable residential neighborhood, this burial ground was no longer in use. After 1851 burials for members of the congregation were moved to Cypress Hills, Queens. In 1897 the West

19th Street synagogue was demolished (to prevent its conversion for other uses) and the congregation relocated to its present building on Central Park West and West 70th Street.

The first Sephardic burial ground, dating from 1656, has vanished. Two other early cemeteries survive: the first remaining graveyard (1683-1828) at 55 St. James Place, opposite Chatham Square in lower Manhattan, and the second (1805-1829) at 72-76 West 11th Street, between Fifth and Sixth Avenues.

Return to Sixth Avenue. Walk south almost to the corner of West 20th Street.

LM19 An English country-style church complex on the northeast corner of West 20th Street remains from the era when fashionable homes still lined Sixth Avenue. The Episcopal **Church of the Holy Communion** (Richard Upjohn, 1844-1845) was consecrated in 1846, in the same year as the architect's Trinity Church downtown at Broadway and Wall Street. The first rector of the church, Reverend William Augustus Muhlenberg, founded the New York Ecclesiological Society, an outgrowth of an evangelical movement in England which looked back to medieval authority as a basis for religious belief. Reflecting the movement's view that the Gothic style was the true architectural expression of Christianity, Upjohn designed the religious complex in the Gothic Revival style.

All of the buildings are constructed of randomly laid brownstone blocks. The church is notable for its asymmetrical design, Gothic detailing, and crenelated corner tower. Within the picturesque grouping is the three-story, peaked-roof Sisters' House (1854) to the left of the church, which sheltered the nation's first Episcopal sisterhood and was the first site of St. Luke's Hospital. Completing the complex are the Parish House and Rectory (1853) on West 20th Street. A plaque to the left of the doorway in the corner tower tells the story of the early history of the church.

In the early 1970s the dwindling congregation merged with two nearby parishes and the buildings were acquired by the drug rehabilitation organization Odyssey House. Facing a fiscal crisis in 1982, Odyssey House sold the buildings to Peter Gatien, a nightclub entrepreneur who, to the horror of many, converted the old church complex into a dance club called Limelight. Unfortunately, this transformation has not benefited these landmark buildings, which currently suffer from neglect.

Cross West 20th Street and Sixth Avenue. Walk south to the middle of the block.

LM20 Directly across Sixth Avenue, on the west side of the block between West 19th and West 20th Streets, is the former **Simpson-Crawford & Simpson**, Nos. 635-649 (William H. Hume & Son, 1900-1902). This luxury establishment catered to the elite carriage trade and displayed high-quality, expensive clothing without price-tags so as not to offend their upper-class patrons. The limestone and brick building rises six stories above a polished granite base and is ornamented with subdued foliate carvings. In contrast to its more highly decorated neighbors, the sedate Beaux-Arts facade is understated and reserved. Simpson-Crawford was not interested in attracting customers from the passing elevated trains since those riders could not afford to shop in the store. A large interior court topped by a dome and a penthouse restaurant designed in the Louis XVI style created a luxurious atmosphere inside. Escalators, among the first to be installed in a department store, were a modern innovation. Simpson-Crawford & Simpson was out of business by World War I and the building was converted to warehouse and manufacturing space. Several businesses and a technical school currently occupy the ground floor.

Continue walking south on Sixth Avenue. Cross West 19th Street and walk a few steps.

LM21 Filling the entire blockfront from West 18th Street to West 19th Street on the west side of Sixth Avenue is a four-story, iron-fronted building, the former **B. Altman** at Nos. 615-629 (D. & J. Jardine, 1876-77 and 1880; William Hume, 1887; Buchman & Fox, 1909-10). The store was constructed in four stages. The first building was designed in the neo-Grec style which originated in France as a machine-age interpretation of classical ornament. It utilized single-line incised designs to create a crisp and modern look. Fashions in clothing might change but, thanks to the technology of cast-iron construction in which original forms could be readily dupli-

Sixth *Avenue elevated railway looking north from the station at West 18th Street, 1890. On the left, B. Altman. Visible in the distance, the domes of Hugh O'Neill's.*

cated, the architectural style of the building remained consistent as it was expanded over a 30-year period.

B. Altman began in the 1860s as a small family-owned store on the Lower East Side. After several changes in location and management, one of the brothers, Benjamin Altman (future art collector and philanthropist), became the sole owner. In 1876 he established the business here. The store cultivated a reputation for attentive service, excellence of merchandise, and the convenience of speedy delivery. B. Altman left the Ladies' Mile in 1906, leading the movement of department stores uptown. The store continued its tradition of offering quality merchandise and service at its location on Fifth Avenue at East 34th Street until closing in 1989, breaking the hearts of countless loyal customers. A branch of the clothing chain Today's Man currently occupies the ground floor of the building.

Note the carefully restored cast-iron front of the former B. Altman building. Its incised detailing is characteristic of the neo-Grec style popular in New York in the 1870s.

Retrace your steps to West 19th Street. Cross Sixth Avenue. Walk toward West 18th Street and stop in the middle of the block.

LM22 Directly across the street, on the east side of Sixth Avenue, the former **Siegel-Cooper**, Nos. 616-632 (DeLemos & Cordes, 1895-1897; addition, 1899), spans the block between West 18th and West 19th Streets. This was the first steel-framed department store in the city and was, at the time of completion, the biggest store in the world. The architects went on to design the present Macy's in midtown, passing on the title of world's largest in 1902. Designed as a grand Beaux-Arts palace, the imposing, ivory-colored brick and terra-cotta structure rises six stories and is half a block deep. Embellishing the spectacular facade are columns, balconies, marble panels, foliate ornament, terra-cotta shields inscribed with the letters "SC," and lions' heads along the cornice. The impressive triple-arched entrance provided a dramatic gateway to the shopper's paradise within.

Unlike most other Sixth Avenue merchants, whose businesses evolved from small dry goods shops in converted houses, Siegel-Cooper burst on the scene when Chicago retailer Henry Siegel expanded his successful company into the New York market. Under one roof shoppers could find a wide variety of merchandise as well as a photo studio, bank, telegraph office, dental parlor, barber shop, a grocery department, a restaurant seating 350 people, and a conservatory selling live plants. In

More than 150,000 eager shoppers, the majority arriving on the elevated trains, jammed Sixth Avenue, when Siegel-Cooper opened on September 12, 1896. The store advertised itself as "The Big Store, A City in Itself" and "Everything Under the Sun."

the center of the main floor a marble-enclosed fountain, with a replica of the statue *The Republic* by Daniel Chester French, became a popular gathering place and "meet me at the fountain" a familiar phrase to New Yorkers.

Siegel-Cooper employed a work force of more than 3,000 and provided its mainly female staff (many still in their teens) with such amenities as an infirmary, a parlor, and a gym. In his short stories, O. Henry described the great emporiums on Ladies' Mile from the viewpoint of the young women who worked in them. In "The Trimmed Lamp," the author compared the department store to a university where working girls educated themselves in the manners, speech, and dress of their well-bred female clientele in the hope of securing a "swell gentleman" as a "matrimonial prize." But in "A Lick-penny Lover," class differences kept eighteen-year-old Maisie, who sold "gents gloves" in "the Biggest Store," from comprehending the proposal of a millionaire suitor.

Siegel-Cooper was sold in 1902 to new owners who also acquired the B. Altman building and unsuccessfully ran an expanded business. After Siegel-Cooper closed its doors in 1917, the once-proud store became warehouse space. Joining in the rebirth of Ladies' Mile, major retailers Bed Bath and Beyond, Filene's Basement, and T.J. Maxx currently share space in the vast building.

Walk to the northwest corner of West 18th street.

LM23 Diagonally across Sixth Avenue at Nos. 604-612 on the southeast corner of West 18th Street is the four-story **Price Building** (Buchman & Fox, 1910-1912). The trim white structure, decorated with lions' heads at the third story and capped by a bracketed metal cornice, originally held lofts and small stores. It has been renovated as the clothing store Old Navy, a division of the Gap.

Cross Sixth Avenue. Walk north toward West 19th Street to the middle of the block.

The entrance of the former Siegel-Cooper is flanked by two tall, fluted bronze columns enriched by decorative bands encircling them at mid-section. The base of the column on the left is inscribed with the name of their designer, Paul E. Cabaret; just below that are the names of the architects of the building, DeLemos & Cordes. You may want to take time to explore the three stores housed in the enormous interior.

The Siegel-Cooper building extends 460 feet along the south side of West 19th Street. The remainder of the block is lined with office and loft buildings; street-level stores are interspersed with former homes converted to commercial use.

Sixth Avenue elevated railway station at West 18th Street.

LM24 Look for the old houses at **No. 29** and **No. 25**; although somewhat altered, they are survivors of a mid-19th-century residential neighborhood.

A Fifth Avenue address has conveyed a distinctive cachet since the 1840s, when New York's wealthiest families built substantial homes and churches along the avenue north of the elegant row houses on Washington Square. By the 1880s, as the city's accelerating economy continued to drive affluent residents north, Fifth Avenue up to Madison Square had developed into a commercial thoroughfare of prestigious hotels, restaurants, retail establishments and office buildings.

Walk north along Sixth Avenue. Cross West 19th Street and turn right. Walk east toward Fifth Avenue.

Stop at the northwest corner of Fifth Avenue and West 19th Street.

LM25 The imposing structure diagonally across the street, at 115 Fifth Avenue once housed the **Arnold Constable & Company Annex** (Griffith Thomas, 1876). The enormous emporium, influenced by Renaissance designs, stretches to Broadway along East 19th Street. Almost a decade after the original marble-faced store on Broadway was completed in 1868, the building was enlarged and its Broadway facade replicated in cast-iron on the Fifth Avenue addition. The building rises five stories with a series of stacked arches and is topped by a two-story, French Second Empire roof.

The company was founded by Aaron Arnold, who opened a small dry goods store in lower Manhattan in 1825. Several years later James Constable married Arnold's daughter Henrietta and was taken in as a partner. Arnold Constable occupied a five-story, white marble commercial palace (which is still standing) at Canal and Mercer Street for 12 years until moving to Broadway.

When the store opened on Ladies' Mile it was the largest of the luxury stores and counted among its patrons the wives of the city's affluent financiers and industrialists. Louise Whitfield Carnegie, Frances Tracy Morgan, Laura Spelman Rockefeller, and First Ladies Mary Todd Lincoln and Frances Folsom Cleveland were frequent shoppers. The elite establishment lived up to its slogan "Everything from Cradle to Grave" by offering children's apparel, women's attire in silk, velvet, lace, and fur as well as clothing suitable for mourning.

In 1914 Arnold Constable moved to its new building on Fifth Avenue and East 40th Street (today the Midtown Branch of the New York Public Library) where it remained in operation until 1975.

The Arnold Constable building stretches along the entire south side of East 19th Street between Fifth Avenue and Broadway.

LM25a Diagonally across the street is the marble-faced Broadway facade of the original **Arnold Constable** at Nos. 881-887 (Griffith Thomas, 1868; alterations, 1872). It was the model for its almost identical Fifth Avenue cast-

Cross Fifth Avenue. Continue walking east on East 19th Street.

Cross Broadway to the northeast corner of East 19th Street.

iron counterpart. In the 1960s, in a far-sighted move to the then-defunct Ladies' Mile, ABC Carpet and Home acquired this building. It currently houses broadloom and design rug departments. (More about ABC later in the tour.)

LM26 The picturesque red-brick former **Gorham Building,** Nos. 889-891 (Edward Hale Kendall, 1883-1884), stands directly across Broadway on the northwest corner of East 19th Street. Ogden and Robert Goelet commissioned this building on property that the family had been acquiring in the area since the 1840s. It was planned as a mixed-use building with bachelor apartments initially occupying six floors above two stories of retail space for the Gorham Company. The building was designed in the

Gorham Building,
c. 1885.

Queen Anne style, inspired by 16th- and 17th-century domestic English architecture, which was deemed especially suited to residential design. Pedimented dormers, Flemish gables, and a steep slate roof with iron cresting animate the roofline. The building is further enlivened by terra-cotta ornament and sandstone trim. Note the sunflower design, characteristic of the Queen Anne style, on the tie rods above the fifth-story windows.

The residential apartments lasted for only a few years. The company was a leading manufacturer of fine silver, with a factory in Rhode Island and as sales expanded it took over the entire building. Such "princely gifts accessible to any purse" as silver tableware, carved punch bowls, goblets, and tea and coffee sets were displayed on the first floor, while the upper stories were devoted to ecclesiastical artwork, engravers, and the hotel and wholesale departments. After the Gorham Company moved to midtown in 1905, the building was converted to lofts and offices. In 1977, in a return to its original character, the upper floors were remodeled as apartments. The ground floor is occupied by Fishs Eddy, a retailer of new and vintage china and glassware.

Walk north up Broadway. Cross East 20th Street to the northeast corner.

LM27 Illuminating the southwest corner of Broadway and East 20th Street diagonally across the intersection is one of the architectural stars of Ladies' Mile, the striking cast-iron-fronted building at No. 901 designed for **Lord & Taylor** (James H. Giles, 1869-1870). With its bold and distinctive corner tower capped by a mansard roof with delicate iron cresting, the building is a particularly fine example of the French Second Empire commercial style popular in New York in the 1860s and 1870s. The many large windows, a modern amenity in the gaslight era, enhance its light and airy appearance. The original store extended south on Broadway and, over the years, expanded several times along East 20th Street.

Samuel Lord's first dry goods store opened in 1826 in lower Manhattan on Catherine Street near the East River docks, where he bought merchandise directly from sailing ships. Within 12 years Lord was joined by his wife's cousin George Washington Taylor. The business moved

The vacant Lord & Taylor building after the firm moved in 1914. The store flourishes today in midtown, one of New York's oldest retailers still in operation.

steadily uptown through a series of stores, arriving at Broadway and East 20th Street as one of the pioneers in the development of Ladies' Mile. Lord & Taylor carried a wide range of quality men's and women's clothing as well as carpets and upholstery for its wealthy customers.

The store boasted an early steam elevator designed as a small room, with a carpeted floor and upholstered seating for its elegant clientele. Its creative Christmas windows (which still delight the public), arranged for holiday enjoyment rather than marketing, set the standard for seasonal retail displays. In 1914 Lord & Taylor left the Ladies' Mile (along with Arnold Constable) and relocated to Fifth Avenue between West 38th and West 39th Streets.

LM28 Two distinctive buildings by McKim, Mead & White stand diagonally across from each other on Broadway but are worlds apart. On the northwest corner of

Look directly across Broadway.

East 20th Street at No. 903-907 is the former **Warren Building** (McKim, Mead & White, 1890-1891), designed for ground-floor stores with lofts and offices above. The highly ornamented structure, inspired by Renaissance models, faced in tan Roman brick rises seven stories capped by an elaborate cornice lined with lions' heads. Conspicuous terra-cotta quoins frame the windows. The facade is ornately detailed with marble and terra cotta to create a dizzying array of acanthus leaf brackets, deco-rated panels, friezes, swags, and rosettes. A marble colonnade that originally graced the ground floor has been removed. Early tenants were upholstery, floor-cov-ering, and lace suppliers. Today's occupants are in the advertising and publishing businesses.

Warren Building, c. 1910.

LM29 On the southeast corner, in stunning contrast to the Warren Building, stands an early commercial structure in modern form. It is the salmon-colored, brick and stone **Goelet Building,** Nos. 894-900 (McKim, Mead & White, 1886-1887; renovations and additions, Maynicke & Franke, 1905-1906), completed three years before the Warren Building was designed. This highly original building was not based on a specific historical style, but was undoubtedly influenced by the contemporary designs of master architect H.H. Richardson in whose Boston office both Charles Follen McKim and Stanford White worked during the 1870s. Comparing the two buildings we can see how, within a few years, McKim, Mead & White turned away from function and originality in their designs, choosing instead an architecture based on Renaissance forms. In contrast to the highly decorated Warren Building, the Goelet Building is understated, relying on gradations of color in the brick, patterned brickwork and intricate designs in the spandrels for decoration.

Cross Broadway to the northwest corner of East 20th Street.

The Goelet Building before devastating alterations in 1905.

A dramatic effect is achieved by the continuous facade which wraps around the corner of East 20th Street. The building is anchored by enormous Romanesque arches at the base. In the mid-section, windows are arranged in vertical strips alternating with brick piers. The structure was originally six stories tall and was capped by an impressive cornice. In 1905 renovations seriously compromised its form when the top story was replaced by an additional five stories. The removal of the cornice some time before 1931 was a further desecration to the integrity of the original design.

LM30 The **McIntyre Building,** 874 Broadway (R. H. Robertson, 1890-1892), rises on the northeast corner of Broadway at East 18th Street. Built with street-level stores

Walk back down Broadway. Cross East 19th Street and walk to the middle of the block.

99

with offices above, the ten-story limestone and brick building is capped by a distinctive square tower with a pyramidal roof and steeply pitched gables.

LM31 The former **W. & J. Sloane** at Nos. 880-886 (William Wheeler Smith, 1881-1882, 1898) is directly across the street. Today it houses ABC Carpet and Home. The retail store rises six stories with a later addition of a nine-story warehouse to the east. This is a straightforward, utilitarian commercial structure with large windows bringing light into the vast interior. The facade is organized in a grid pattern with horizontals of gray stone and verticals of red brick expressing the essential structure of the building. Restrained ornament enlivens the facade above the rough-cut stone base and sizable display windows. Mythic creatures and birds nestle in the carved capitals of the brick pilasters. The year of construction can be found in terra-cotta Roman numerals in a panel high above the main entrance.

William Sloane, a young Scottish weaver, opened a carpeting and floor cloth shop on lower Broadway in 1843, and his brother John joined the business several years later. When William purchased the entire collection of Oriental rugs displayed at the Philadelphia Exposition in 1876, W. & J. Sloane became the first store in the city to sell Oriental rugs. All of upper-class New York seemed to be carpeted by W. & J. Sloane including the homes of the Astors, Morgans, and Vanderbilts. The company supplied the carpeting for the original Waldorf-Astoria Hotel, the first Metropolitan Opera House, ocean liners, and the coronation of Czar Nicholas II. In 1912 W. & J. Sloane joined the exodus of retailers to more fashionable addresses in midtown.

In the early 1980s ABC Carpet and Home crossed Broadway, keeping the former Arnold Constable store where it had been for 20 years and expanding into the old W. & J. Sloane building. Following in the footsteps of its illustrious predecessor, ABC used the grand space to display domestic and imported rugs and carpets. Now run by the third and fourth generations, the family business traces its origins to the current president's grandfa-

Cross Broadway at E. 19th Street.

The east side of
Broadway between
East 18th and East
19th Streets, early
1900s. The McIntyre
Building is at the
right. On the left, W.
& J. Sloane.

ther, Sam Weinrib, who in 1897 began peddling used
carpet and linoleum from a pushcart on the Lower East
Side. In recent years ABC Carpet and Home has transformed the former W. & J. Sloane store into a multiplex
stage set for consumer theater, where merchandise from
over 2,000 international vendors creates an atmosphere
of domestic abundance reminiscent of the Victorian era.

Note the imaginative displays in the large show windows before you enter ABC through the wood-paneled
vestibule. The Parlour Cafe at the rear of the store on the
lower mezzanine offers a varied menu in relaxed surroundings, and restrooms can be found nearby.

Map of Chelsea, 1869.

Chelsea Walk

Introduction

The complex identity of Chelsea is rooted in its origins as rural farmland developed as a planned urban community. Commercial growth later expanded its original boundaries from the historic core. In 1750 founding father Captain Thomas Clarke, a retired British military officer, bought a tract of land from Jacob Somerindyke extending approximately from the present West 20th Street to West 28th Street, from Fitzroy Road (Eighth Avenue) to the Hudson River. Clarke called his waterfront estate "Chelsea," either alluding to the riverside Chelsea section of London or, by some accounts, naming it after the Chelsea Royal Hospital, a facility for retired soldiers on the banks of the Thames designed by Christopher Wren in the late 17th century. It is likely that the original meaning of "Chelsea" is "chalk wharf," referring to the traces of that shell-like stone found in the Thames.

The essential character of Chelsea was shaped by Clarke's grandson, Clement Clarke Moore, classical scholar, philanthropist, and sometime poet. In 1813 Moore inherited the portion of the family property south of West 24th Street including an extension to West 19th Street. In the 1830s Moore, along with builder James N. Wells, turned to real estate development and urban planning. Residential lots were laid out on the Chelsea farm and sold with restrictive deeds specifying construction and design standards. Various restrictions were in force for different blocks, but all of them had specifications for size and materials, open space, quality of construction and the compatibility of design of each house with others on the row. The strict deed covenants prohibited commercial use and alleys, thus eliminating stables and back houses. From the mid-1830s through the 1850s Chelsea was built up with mansions, large town houses, and row houses in the Greek Revival, Italianate and Anglo-Italianate styles, with ample front yards on tree-lined streets. In 1845 London Terrace, a grand row of town houses, was built on West 23rd Street stretching from Ninth to Tenth Avenues across from the Moore family home. Although Moore had envisioned Chelsea as an enclave for the elite, it instead developed as an upper-middle-class neighborhood. The fashionably affluent stayed away, put off by its far-west location.

Moore laid out a residential square from West 20th Street to West 21st Street, between Ninth and Tenth Avenues, and in 1829 made a gift of the 60 central building lots to the General Theological Seminary. Chelsea Square North and Chelsea Square South facing the Seminary are considered some of the finest row house blocks in the city. Moore also donated the land for and was involved in the design of St. Peter's Church on West 20th Street between Eighth and Ninth Avenues. The church complex is composed of the original 1832 Greek Revival Chapel, a Gothic Revival church completed in 1838, and an adjacent Victorian Gothic Parish Hall built in 1871.

Although London Terrace was demolished in the 1920s (and replaced by the apartment complex of that name), the core blocks of Chelsea remain remarkably intact. In 1970 the New York City Landmarks Preservation Commission designated the **Chelsea Historic District;** an extension was approved in 1981. The landmark district stretches from West 19th to portions of West 23rd Streets between Tenth Avenue and mid-block to Eighth Avenue. The current boundaries of Chelsea stretch from West 14th to about West 30th Street from Sixth Avenue to the Hudson River.

Chelsea's commercial character developed in the 1840s with the construction of the Hudson River Railroad freight line close to waterfront piers, spurring the development of industry. The docks brought shipping and, later, transatlantic ocean liners to Chelsea. Factories and warehouses rose on streets outside of the original residential blocks and tenements went up to house the growing work force. Hundreds of these deteriorated buildings were later demolished north of West 23rd Street for the Elliot and Fulton public housing projects and the union-sponsored moderate-income Penn South co-ops. The neighborhood has been home to a diverse ethnic population of Irish, Scottish, French, German, Italian, Greek, Eastern European, African, Caribbean, Asian, and Hispanic ancestry. In recent years the immigrant presence has diminished as professionals, some with young children and many in the gay and lesbian community, have begun to move into the area, energizing the local economy.

Chelsea's fun-loving personality came on the scene after the Civil War, when theaters and other entertainment spilled over from Broadway onto West 23rd Street and along Sixth Avenue. In the early 1900s, before the film industry moved to Hollywood, production companies cranked out movies using warehouses and an old armory for studio space. Songwriters and music publishers created the cacophony of Tin Pan Alley, centered around West 28th Street from Sixth Avenue to Broadway. The fur industry, the flower market, the photo district and the antique trade have all made niches for themselves in modern Chelsea. Off-Broadway theater, dance companies, and music clubs flourish. In recent years major galleries have moved from SoHo and Tribeca into converted warehouses and garages at the edge of Chelsea in the West 20s, creating a new center in the city for the contemporary art scene.

Tour

CH1 The **Muhlenberg Branch of the New York Public Library** at No. 209 (Carrère & Hastings, 1906) is one of the Carnegie libraries, a network of 67 branch libraries funded by a gift of $5.2 million given in 1901 by retired industrialist Andrew Carnegie. The libraries were freestanding masonry structures designed by prominent architects in various classical styles with restrained exterior ornament. The interiors, planned in consultation with librarians, were functional, light, and airy. This compact, three-story building faced in limestone was designed in the Renaissance Revival style by the architects of the Central Research Library on Fifth Avenue. It

The tour begins on the north side of West 23rd Street just west of Seventh Avenue.

was named for William Augustus Muhlenberg, a prominent Chelsea clergyman who was the first pastor of the Church of the Holy Communion on Sixth Avenue and West 20th Street. Muhlenberg's collection of books formed the core holdings of the library. (See the **Ladies' Mile Tour.**)

Walk a few steps west.

CH2 The ten-story **McBurney Y.M.C.A.** (Parish & Schroeder, 1903-1904) at No. 215 was named for Robert Ross McBurney, an Irish immigrant who came to New York in 1845 and was an early leader in the Y.M.C.A. movement. The community-based service organization offers programs emphasizing education, health, and recreation for youth and adults. It operates a gym, swimming pool, and co-ed hotel for 279 residents. In 1906 brothers Homer and Charles Pace established a night-school course in accounting, economics, and law at the McBurney Y as an extension of their one room business school on Park Row (now Pace University). A chance meeting between Charles E. Merrill and Edmund C. Lynch in the Y swimming pool led to the formation of their financial partnership in 1913. More recent members have included Andy Warhol, Edward Albee, and Al Pacino. In the lobby Cafe Global, staffed by advanced students in the English language program, is open to the public.

CH3 Look across West 23rd Street at the red-brick building with sunflower-studded iron balconies. It is the legendary **Chelsea Hotel,** one of the great cultural landmarks of the city. Built as Chelsea Apartments (Hubert, Pirsson & Co., 1883-1884), an early cooperative apartment house, it became a hotel in 1905, renting out about half of its units to long-term residents. Dormers and tall chimneys animate the roofline of the 12-story building. The sunflower motif and small-paned windows (some with surviving stained glass) are typical of the Queen Anne style.

The Chelsea Hotel stands as a mecca for creative spirits, with its guest register almost a "Who's Who" of literature and the arts. The hotel has welcomed such lumi-

The Chelsea Hotel
at the turn of the
century. The tower on
the left is Westminster
Presbyterian Church.
At the right, the
Third Reformed
Presbyterian Church,
now Congregation
Emunath Israel.

naries as painters John Sloan, Willem de Kooning, Jackson Pollack, and Larry Rivers. Actresses Sarah Bernhardt and Lillian Russell stayed here while starring in local theaters. Composer Virgil Thomson lived in the hotel in exotic splendor for 50 years. The curious still ask to see the room in which Sid Vicious, bass player for the punk rock group the Sex Pistols, stabbed his girlfriend Nancy Spungen to death in 1978.

Above all it is the writers who have given the Chelsea its creative mystique. In the 1880s Mark Twain held court in the opulent dining room. Among other literary lodgers were Eugene O'Neill, Tennessee Williams, Mary McCarthy, and Brendan Behan. Thomas Wolfe spent his last months at the hotel and left behind manuscripts for

Return to Seventh Avenue. Cross West 23rd Street and walk to the Chelsea Hotel.

The Web and the Rock and *You Can't Go Home Again*. William Burroughs' *Naked Lunch* and Arthur Clarke's *2001* were written here. Arthur Miller wrote three plays while living at the hotel. Twenty-year resident Edgar Lee Masters composed a long poem celebrating the glories of what is no doubt the most intriguing hotel in New York.

Works of past and present residents are on display in the lobby-turned-art-gallery. Before you go inside note the plaques around the entrance that memorialize some of the hotel's celebrated personalities. The most poignant honors Welsh poet Dylan Thomas "who lived and labored last here...and from here sailed out to die."

CH4 Next door at No. 263 stands the Gothic Revival former Third Reformed Presbyterian Church (1855), now **Congregation Emunath Israel,** "faith of Israel," (renovations, Abraham Grossman, 1951). The Orthodox Jewish congregation was organized in 1863 on West 18th Street, later moving to 301 West 29th Street before relocating here in 1920. Tablets of the Ten Commandments surmount the entrance and the words "Torah," "prayer," and "benevolence" are inscribed on the exterior. The synagogue is a center for Orthodox Jewish life in Chelsea and has developed model programs for the Jewish homeless, offering kosher meals, job placement, and counseling services.

Continue walking along West 23rd Street. Cross Eighth Avenue to the southwest corner.

CH5 The **Grand Opera House** stood on the northwest corner of Eighth Avenue and West 23rd Street. When it opened in 1868 as Pike's Opera House it was devoted to Italian opera. Lighter entertainment was introduced the following year after the theater was acquired by financiers Jim Fisk and Jay Gould. While audiences attended theatricals downstairs, the partners manipulated Erie Railroad stock and plotted to corner the gold market from their plush offices upstairs. Josie Mansfield, Fisk's mistress, presided over extravagant galas in the ornate ballroom. Fisk's life ended dramatically in 1872 when, at age 37, he was fatally shot by a rival for Josie's affection. His spectacular funeral was held in the Grand Opera House as the closing act in a flamboyant life. The theater

continued to operate under Jay Gould and other producers such as George M. Cohan and Sam Harris. In the early 1900s the top floors were converted to offices and a rehearsal space; Fred Astaire and his sister Adele practiced in a dance studio in the former ballroom. In 1917, the theater switched to films and vaudeville. It was demolished in 1960.

The Grand Opera House in 1937 in a photograph by Berenice Abbott.

CH6 Penn Station South (Herman Jessor, 1962), now called **Penn South,** is a moderate-income cooperative development of 2,820 apartments sponsored by the International Ladies Garment Workers Union. The ten, 21-story red-brick apartment buildings stand in a park-like setting from West 23rd Street to West 29th Street between Eighth Avenue and Ninth Avenue. Tenants uprooted from their deteriorating housing on the site were given priority for apartments in the new buildings along with I.L.G.W.U. members. Construction costs were financed by the union with additional city, state, and federal funding.

Walk to the middle of the block and look across West 23rd Street.

President John F. Kennedy at the dedication of Penn South, May 19, 1962. At left shaking hands, is Governor Nelson Rockefeller. To Kennedy's right is David Dubinsky, president of the I.L.G.W.U. sponsor of the project. At far right, George Meany, president of the A.F.L.-C.I.O.

Led by its dynamic president David Dubinsky for more than 30 years, the I.L.G.W.U. was in the forefront of social welfare reform and succeeded in bringing a standard 35-hour week to workers toiling in the sweatshops. Although occupancy in Penn South was not limited to union members, the majority of early residents were employed in the nearby garment district and found the location convenient. Most of the current residents are elderly, many of them original occupants living on fixed incomes.

Located within the clearance site, but spared from demolition in an enlightened act of preservation, are the Episcopal Church of the Holy Apostles (Minard Lafever, 1848) at 300 Ninth Avenue on the southeast corner of West 28th Street and the Saint Columba Roman Catholic Church (1845), Rectory (1848), and Parochial School (Thomas H. Poole, 1911) at 331-343 West 25th Street. Lafever's church, an outstanding example of early Italianate design, has recently been reconstructed after a catastrophic fire caused extensive damage to the structure. For the past 15 years, the Holy Apostles Soup Kitchen has operated an extensive program serving meals to the poor of the city. Perhaps the most famous student to attend St. Columba's Parochial School was actor-comedian Whoopi Goldberg (then known as Caryn Johnson), who lived in public housing at Tenth Avenue and West 26th Street. Her dramatic talents were nurtured in a theater program for pre-teens at the Hudson Guild, a settlement house at 441 West 26th Street, which has been serving the Chelsea community for more than 100 years.

CH7 New York's oldest real estate firm, originally James N. Wells' Sons, now **Stribling-Wells & Gay** is located at No. 340. James N. Wells, a successful carpenter-builder in Greenwich Village, founded the business in 1819. He is known as the builder of the Episcopal Church of St. Luke-in-the-Fields on Hudson Street (1822). In 1833 Wells moved his office and home from Hudson Street to 401 West 21st Street. Two years later he constructed one of his many buildings in Chelsea, a mansion at 414-416 West 22nd Street (both to come on the tour). Wells worked with Clement Clarke Moore as manager of the Chelsea estate, developing the old farm into a new residential neighborhood.

Continue walking along West 23rd Street.

Wells died in 1860 but the company remained in the family until the early 1900s, and then was run by a series of owners. The firm moved into this four-story 1849 brick row house soon after it was renovated and given an elegant neo-Classical front (Paul C. Hunter, 1933). In the 1970s owner Paul Gay added his name to the company's. The present name dates to 1989 when the firm was acquired by Stribling & Associates, a leading brokerage headed by Elizabeth Stribling. Step inside the handsome town house for a look at the display of historic documents and photos on the walls of the entryway.

CH8 The route of the earliest urban rapid transit system in America ran along **Ninth Avenue.** The first elevated train line in the United States began operating in 1868 with a small locomotive pulled by a fixed cable on tracks

Continue walking west. Cross Ninth Avenue to the southwest corner of West 23rd Street.

Looking south under the Ninth Avenue elevated railway station from West 25th Street, 1915.

above Greenwich Street from the Battery to Dey Street in lower Manhattan. By 1870 the line was extended to the vicinity of West 14th Street, and from there along Ninth Avenue to West 29th Street. In 1872 cable was replaced by noisy steam-driven trains of the New York Elevated Railway Company which chugged on tracks above Ninth Avenue until 1940.

CH9 London Terrace (Farrar & Watmaugh, 1929-1930) fills the block from West 23rd to West 24th Street, Ninth Avenue to Tenth Avenue. It is on the site of its namesake, a row of town houses on the north side of West 23rd Street which stretched from Ninth Avenue to Tenth Avenue (Alexander Jackson Davis, 1848). The row was inspired by similar rows in London (the British call them "terraces") which created monumental, classical streetscapes. The individual four-story houses, on lots sold with restrictive deeds by Clement Clarke Moore, were set behind large front yards and unified by a continuous line of pilasters, suggesting a colonnade.

As the affluent moved uptown in the late 19th century, the houses were subdivided, with cheap rents for the decaying structures attracting artists and writers. Poet

112

Edward Arlington Robinson lived in an upstairs back room at No. 450 in the early 1900s. Author Van Wyck Brooks recalled the mildewed odors of the furnished rooms he rented in 1910. The first London Terrace and a similar row called Chelsea Cottages on West 24th Street were demolished in 1929, making way for the present London Terrace.

When the huge residential complex opened in the Depression, tenants were greeted by doormen outfitted as London bobbies in what was advertised as "the world's largest apartment house." Over 4,000 people live in the development, in 670 co-op apartments in the four corner towers and 1,000 studio and one-bedroom, rent-regulated and market-rate apartments in the ten middle buildings. The 16-story, block-long, street wall of reddish-orange brick is punctuated by several handsome entrances. Variations of color and texture, ornamental brickwork, and Romanesque-inspired detailing enliven the facade. The complex boasts a roof with stunning views of the Hudson and a 75-foot swimming pool. Not visible from the street is a private central garden for the exclusive use of residents.

In recent years London Terrace has been dubbed "the fashion projects." Located close to the garment district

The first London Terrace, just before demolition, looking west from the Ninth Avenue railway station at West 23rd Street, 1929.

and Chelsea's photo studios, the complex has attracted celebrity residents Isaac Mizrahi, Todd Oldham, and Annie Leibovitz, as well as other prominent designers, photographers, editors, models, and stylists in the fashion industry.

Continue along West 23rd Street.

CH10 Look for the tiny plaque just before the entrance to No. 420 marking the approximate site of **Chelsea House,** the Clarke and Moore family home and the birthplace of Clement Clarke Moore (1779-1863). The house was built in 1777 by his maternal grandmother, Mistress Molly Clarke, widow of Captain Thomas Clarke, after fire destroyed the original homestead nearby. Moore's mother, Charity Clarke, was married to the Reverend Benjamin Moore, one of the city's most-revered clergy-

Portrait of Clement Clarke Moore by Daniel Huntington, 1851.

men. As rector of Trinity
Church he administered
last rites to Alexander
Hamilton in 1804, served
as the second Episcopal
Bishop of New York, and
was President of Kings
College (now Columbia
University).

Clement Clarke Moore
grew up in and later
inherited Chelsea House.
After his marriage in 1813
his parents deeded him the southern portion of the original Chelsea estate along with a small additional piece
encompassing all the land from the present West 19th
Street to West 24th Street between Eighth Avenue and
the Hudson River. Moore turned the estate into a tree-
lined residential neighborhood with rows of gracious
houses set back from the street by front yards. He
donated a square block to the General Theological Seminary (still to come on this tour), of which he was a fac-
ulty member. Ironically, this notable urban planner,
philanthropist, theological scholar, and linguist is best
known for his poem "A Visit from St. Nicholas," popularly called "'Twas the night before Christmas," written
for his children in 1822.

*An 1850s daguerreo-
type of Chelsea House
by Clement Clarke
Moore's cousin,
Nathaniel Fish Moore.*

You are now entering the **Chelsea Historic District,**
on one of the last blocks to be developed on the Chelsea
estate. In 1853, at age 74, Clement Clarke Moore left
Chelsea House (on the site of Nos. 422 and 424) to live
nearby with his daughter. The demolition of the family
home soon followed, making way for the row houses on
the south side of West 23rd Street extending to Tenth
Avenue, along with a similar row on the north side of
West 22nd Street.

*Walk a few steps
along West 23rd
Street.*

CH11 All of these handsome four- and five-story row
houses were built between 1854 and 1857 on then-fash-
ionable West 23rd Street across from the first London
Terrace. Over the years, as the one-family dwellings

were subdivided into apartments and rooming houses, the buildings began to deteriorate. In the 1980s **Nos. 428-444** and **No. 450** were renovated into modern cooperative apartments (Beyer Blinder Belle, 1982) with such amenities as wood-burning fireplaces and large private terraces and gardens. The development is called Fitzroy Place after a country road in colonial Chelsea (named for Lord Fitzroy, one of the Crown's representatives to the Colonies) which ran roughly along the present Eighth Avenue. The conversions, along with replanting of the front yards and installation of 19th-century replica lampposts, have brought back the flavor of old Chelsea to West 23rd Street.

This was solid, middle-class housing built by merchants and dealers in lumber and iron. Here you can see at first-hand the realization of Clement Clarke Moore's design standards. All of the residences are similar in construction and are set back from the street behind front yards framed with cast-iron railings.

Although several of the houses were built individually and others in groups of two or more, the row presents a unified appearance. Most of the houses are four stories, faced with brownstone or brick, and have segmental arched lintels and sill brackets. Many have cast-iron railings fronting the parlor floor-windows. An almost continuous line of wide-bracketed cornices links the row. Some of the houses were built with low steps and English basements in the Anglo-Italianate style; others had high stoops in the Italianate style. In 1929 the stoops were removed for a planned widening of West 23rd Street which was never carried out.

Continue walking along West 23rd Street.

CH11 a-k **Nos. 428 and 430,** built as three, 16½-feet-wide, two-bay brownstones, have been converted to two wider buildings. Although most of the houses on the row are faced with brownstone, the three at **Nos. 434, 436, and 438** have brick facades above rusticated brownstone basements. **No. 448** retains much of its original appearance. Note the fine carved entrance decorated with a shell design on the segmental arched pediment supported by carved acanthus-leaf brackets. The rebuilt

high stoop leads to the original paneled wooden doors. There were nine identical houses beginning at **No. 454** that have been modified over the years. **Nos. 462 and 464** survive with many features intact while **No. 466** is almost entirely altered. **No. 468** has been restored and the stoop rebuilt.

CH12 The rusted iron overhead structure spanning West 23rd Street is a portion of an old elevated freight line of Conrail, completed in 1934 to replace unsafe grade-level tracks that ran along Tenth Avenue. The surface line was the Hudson River Railroad, established in the 1840s, running along the shoreline to a terminal at Chambers and Hudson Streets. In Chelsea the shoreline ran along Tenth Avenue (everything west is landfill), sometimes called "Death Avenue" because of the frequent fatal street accidents. For years after the last overhead freight train ran in 1980, transportation planners have been considering, and railroad buffs advocating, an electrified light-rail line along the west side of Manhattan.

CH13 Look north across Eleventh Avenue at the **Starrett-Lehigh Building** (Russell G. Cory and Walter M. Cory and Yasuo Matsui, 1930-1931). The enormous 19-story structure, designed as a warehouse and freight terminal, fills the block between West 26th and West 27th Streets, Eleventh and Twelfth Avenues. A dramatic exterior encloses a rugged, blue-collar interior. Ribbons of strip windows, brick spandrels and concrete bands wrap around the curvilinear frame to create a stunning vision

Looking north on Tenth Avenue from West 24th Street, 1915.

Continue walking along West 23rd Street. Cross Tenth Avenue.

Continue walking on West 23rd Street. Stop on the southeast corner of Eleventh Avenue.

Chelsea Piers, 7 A.M., April 19, 1912. A crowd awaits the arrival of the Cunard liner Carpathia carrying survivors of the Titanic disaster.

of modern architecture. Originally rising above tracks of the Lehigh Valley Railroad, the building has huge elevators that can hold complete loads of railroad boxcars or entire tractor-trailers. Current tenants are industrial, printing, and art-related businesses with future office conversion anticipated. Starrett-Lehigh was the inspiration for a number of striking office buildings nationwide, notably Frank Lloyd Wright's Johnson Wax Building in Racine, Wisconsin and the Look Building in mid-town by Emery Roth & Sons.

CH14 Across six lanes of traffic, stretching south from West 23rd Street to West 17th Street are the Chelsea Piers, four huge waterfront piers (Warren & Wetmore, 1902-1910) that have been transformed into the **Chelsea Piers Sports and Entertainment Complex** (renovations, Butler Rogers Baskett, 1995). Once they were ports for luxury transatlantic liners, the destination for the Titanic on her maiden voyage, and the departure point for the Lusitania on her final voyage. The rotting piers were leased from New York State by developers Roland W. Betts, Tom A. Bernstein, and David A. Tewksbury, and were given a $100 million make-over to create the enormous commercial recreational center. Three giant murals (John Clem Clarke) punctuate the continuous corrugated metal wall extending from West 17th Street to West 22nd Street.

Cross Eleventh Avenue at the traffic light at West 23rd Street.

CH15 Plans are underway to integrate the small, partly paved **Thomas F. Smith Park** (named for a Tammany politician) into Chelsea Waterside Park (Thomas Balsley, designer), an imaginatively designed, substantially expanded public space long championed by neighborhood activists. The new park will open public access to the waterfront which has been closed off for more than a century by commercial development. The 2.5 acres of lawns and plantings, ball field, basketball court, children's play area, dog run, and food concessions will stretch from West 22nd Street to West 24th Street, Eleventh Avenue to the West Side Highway. A street-level pedestrian promenade, designed with visual markers as a Chelsea historic walk, will begin at Eleventh Avenue and cross to the west side of the highway at West 23rd Street. Chelsea Waterside Park will connect to Hudson River Park, with its recreational facilities and pedestrian and bicycle paths, that presently stretches from Battery Park to Chambers Street. Future plans envision a shoreline green strip extending to 59th Street.

Look for the narrow pedestrian walkway between the traffic barriers leading to Chelsea Piers. Stop in the Chelsea Piers office (next to the public restrooms) to pick up brochures describing the vast athletic facilities. Available are indoor running tracks, a rock-climbing wall, swimming pool, basketball and volley ball courts, and a boxing ring in the Sports Center; gymnastics, soccer, lacrosse, field hockey at the Field House; a state-of-the-art driving range at the Golf Club; ice skating at the Sky Rinks, and outdoor Roller Rinks. The Maritime Center offers harbor cruises, a sailing school, and dockage. Also housed in the giant complex are six sound stages for TV and film production at the Silver Screen Studios, a studio for fashion photography, and several restaurants and shops.

Walk south on Eleventh Avenue. Carefully cross Twelfth Avenue at the traffic light.

Take some time to explore the facilities. Don't miss the wall of giant historic photos south of the gym shop. Then walk to the small public-access riverside area that

Retrace your steps
and cross Eleventh
Avenue at the traf-
fic light at West
23rd Street. Do
not be tempted to
sprint through the
busy streams of
traffic in the mid-
dle of the block.
Walk south on
Eleventh Avenue.
Cross West 22nd
Street and turn
left.

will be substantially extended when the waterfront park
is built. Ocean liners, freighters, and tugboats once filled
the busy waters of the Hudson. Riverboats and ferries to
New Jersey docked at the foot of West 23rd Street. Today
the view is more tranquil, despite the passing of an occa-
sional sightseeing vessel.

CH16 The gritty block of former stables, warehouses,
auto repair shops, and garages along West 22nd Street
from Tenth Avenue to Eleventh Avenue has been reborn
as a sophisticated showplace for contemporary art. In
recent years, as major galleries have moved into converted spaces, much of the art scene has shifted from
SoHo to the western edge of Chelsea.

The **Dia Center for the Arts** at 548 West 22nd Street,
housed in a converted warehouse (renovations, Richard
Gluckman, 1987) led the movement. Founded in 1974,
Dia (from the Greek meaning "through") serves as a
conduit for the exhibition of contemporary visual art at
sites in the city and nationwide. Artwork in the Dia permanent collection focuses on Pop, Minimal, Earth Art,
and Conceptual works from the 1960s to the 1980s.

The exhibitions at this site present long-term, large-
scale projects of one artist on each floor of the four-story
building. The center is open from noon to 6:00 P.M.,
Thursday through Sunday, with an admission charge of
$3.00. Dia is closed in the summer. Before you go inside,
take a look at the installation by German conceptual artist
Joseph Beuys along the sidewalk. Titled *7000 Oaks*, the
line of various kinds of trees each with its own basalt
stone, is an extension of an ongoing Earth Art project
begun by the artist in 1982 in Germany.

Make it a point to go up to the roof of the Dia Center
for views of the city and to see the Rooftop Urban Park
Project designed by Dan Graham. There you can experience the site-specific sculpture *Two-Way Mirror Cylinder
Inside Cube* by Graham in collaboration with Moji Baratloo
and Clifton Balch. The work is a pavilion of mirrored

Exit the Dia and
walk east on West
22nd Street.

glass which you can enter. It offers a unique view of the
urban scene. Also on the roof is a coffee shop showing
videos related to the installation.

CH17 Across the street at **No. 545** is a former auto repair garage (renovations, John Grupp, 1993) converted to additional exhibition space for the Dia Center.

CH18 Down the block at **Nos. 528-530** (Seth H. Bevins, 1893) you will find art galleries in a converted public stable.

CH19 No. 525 (W. W. Howe, 1893) is the six-story red-brick **Spears Building**, named for a furniture company that once occupied the 19th-century warehouse. It was recently renovated (Arpad Baska, 1996-1997) and contains 30 luxury loft-style apartments, including six penthouse units with private roof decks. You may want to take time to visit the galleries on the ground floor as well as others on the block and around the corner on West 21st Street.

Continue walking east under the overhead tracks. Cross Tenth Avenue to the northeast corner of West 22nd Street.

CH20 The sleek, stainless-steel **Empire Diner** looks as if it might have glided along railroad tracks on Tenth Avenue before pulling into the corner of West 22nd Street. In reality the black and chrome Art Deco eatery was manufactured by the Fodero Dining Car Company and brought here in 1929. Diners began as working-class horse-drawn lunch wagons and evolved into converted trolley cars and railroad cars at permanent sites. In the 1920s the glamour of streamlined dining cars on such trains as the Twentieth Century Limited fueled the growth of specialized diner manufacturers. Among the celebrity patrons of the Empire have been Franklin D. Roosevelt, Charles Lindbergh, Babe Ruth, Albert Einstein, Barbra Streisand, and Madonna. A small metal sculpture of the namesake Empire State Building tops the rounded roofline. The interior features a shiny winged clock above the counter, the trademark of the Fodero Company.

Walk east on the north side of West 22nd Street.

CH21 Directly across West 22nd Street on the southeast corner is **Clement Clarke Moore Park** (Paul Friedberg, 1968), a small, multi-level urban haven offering shady trees, benches, and imaginative playground areas. It is curious that no other public space or street in the neighborhood memorializes the developer who shaped old Chelsea. In lower Manhattan, North Moore Street is named in honor of his father, the Reverend Benjamin Moore.

CH22 The north side of West 22nd Street between Ninth and Tenth Avenues was developed after Chelsea House was demolished in 1854. The houses were designed in the fashionable Italianate or Anglo-Italianate styles and retain many of their original characteristics. **Nos. 477-457** were remodeled as co-op apartments for Fitzroy Place in 1982, along with similar houses on West 23rd Street seen earlier in the tour.

Continue walking east.

This building at 436 West 22nd Street was home to actor Edwin Forrest and later, furniture designer Christian Herter.

CH23 Of the four Greek Revival mansions built on the south side of West 22nd Street facing the family home of Clement Clarke Moore, two survive in substantially altered form. The four-story brick dwelling at **No. 436** was built in 1835. The stoop has been removed and the entrance, which was originally flanked by fluted Doric columns supporting a heavy entablature, has been redone. Edwin Forrest, the renowned American actor, lived here from 1838 to 1849. He is remembered as the catalyst for the bloody Astor Place Riot which took place on May 10, 1849. Thousands of Forrest's fans, driven by nativist sentiment, attacked the Astor Place Opera House where English actor William Macready was appearing in a rival production of *Macbeth*. Militia from a nearby armory opened fire on the crowd, estimated at 10,000 to 20,000, killing more than 20 rioters and injuring at least 150. A later owner was noted designer Christian Herter, who lived here from 1871 to 1876. The firm of Herter Brothers crafted exquisite, museum-quality furniture by hand for such millionaire patrons as Jay Gould, William H. Vanderbilt, and J.P. Morgan. In 1945 the private house was converted to apartments.

One of the several homes of James N. Wells in Chelsea, 414 West 22nd Street, 1903.

CH24 The other mansion, **No. 414**, was built in 1835 for James N. Wells and, at 44 feet wide, is the largest surviving Greek Revival dwelling in Manhattan. After 30 years, it was given a face-lift (1864-1866) and remodeled in the Italianate style. The parlor-floor windows and mansard roof with dormers and cornice remain from that make-over, but the arched doorway, entablature, window lintels and moldings, and balcony have disappeared. Wells lived here from 1835 to 1841 when he moved to another home, at 162 Ninth Avenue (later on this tour); he came back in 1855 and remained until his death in 1860. The mansion became a home for the aged, was acquired by the Salvation Army, and then remodeled for apartments.

Retrace your steps and begin walking back to Tenth Avenue.

CH25 a-c The south side of the street was developed in the 1830s and 1840s with Greek Revival houses. Although many have been considerably altered or destroyed, several retain their essential character. **No. 444** (1835-1836) and **No. 450** (c. 1835), with their attic windows in the frieze board and decorative iron-work, reveal much of their original design. Standing side by side just before the park are two houses built in 1854. **No. 458**, with its high stoop and basement below ground level, is in the Italianate style and **No. 460** in the Anglo-Italianate-style, with a few steps leading to the English basement slightly above street level.

Continue to Tenth Avenue. Turn left and walk to the northeast corner of West 21st Street.

CH26 Across the street at 193 Tenth Avenue is the Roman Catholic **Church of Our Guardian Angel** and a combined school and rectory building (John Van Pelt, 1930-1931). The parish was established to serve the large number of seamen and longshoremen who worked on the docks along the Hudson River. In 1888 the first church opened in a trio of renovated houses at 511, 513, and 515 West 23rd Street, west of Tenth Avenue. The present religious complex was financed by the New York Central Railroad as a replacement for the old church buildings demolished for construction of the elevated freight railway line (portions of which we have just seen). Constructed of brick and limestone, the church and adjoining buildings are in the Sicilian Romanesque style inspired by the Cathedral of Ritente and the Church of San Pietro in the Puglia district of southern Italy. Above the marble panels is a particularly fine hand-carved limestone frieze depicting Biblical scenes separated by angels standing guard. In the tympanum above the entrance is a carved figure of Christ surrounded by the emblems of the four Evangelists.

CH27 This block of West 21st Street from Ninth Avenue to Tenth Avenue is known as Chelsea Square North. Chelsea Square, bounded by West 20th and West 21st Streets between Ninth and Tenth Avenues, is the peaceful setting for the **General Theological Seminary** of the Episcopal Church. Established in 1817, the seminary's first

classes were held in 1819 in lower Manhattan at St.
Paul's Chapel of Trinity Church. Ten years later the seminary moved to Chelsea Square on some sixty lots
donated by Clement Clarke Moore from his family
estate. Although Moore did not follow in his father's
steps to become a clergyman, he did serve as professor
of Biblical Learning at the Seminary and was an authority on classical literature and languages. Alas, he is better
known for his poem about St. Nicholas than for his
Hebrew lexicon.

The Seminary is a residential institution preparing
men and women for the Episcopal ministry. Visible on
West 21st Street are the rear elevations of buildings
along the northern edge of the campus. Most of the
Seminary buildings are constructed of dark brick with
brownstone and pressed-brick trim. They were erected
between 1883 and 1902 from the designs of architect
Charles Coolidge Haight, commissioned by Dean

Eugene Augustus Hoffman. Haight's master plan for the seminary included academic and office buildings, dormitories, a dining hall, a library, and a chapel. Hoffman Hall, the large building on the southeast corner of Tenth Avenue and West 21st Street, holds a gymnasium and a refectory in a grand, oak-paneled medieval space dominated by a baronial fireplace.

CH27a Rising 161 feet over the middle of the block is the square bell-tower of the **Chapel of the Good Shepherd** (Charles Coolidge Haight, 1886-1888), modeled after Oxford's Magdalen Tower. (More about the Seminary and the church later in the tour.) Chelsea Square North and South are handsome 19th-century residential blocks. Look down at the impressive streetscape along West 21st Street before viewing the individual houses.

Begin walking east on the north side of West 21st Street.

CH28 a-g The Italianate row at **Nos. 473-465** conforms to design covenants decreed by Clement Clarke Moore. The five houses of red brick trimmed with brownstone, all constructed in 1853, are set back behind front yards framed with cast-iron railings to create a dignified row. Note the cruciform paneled doors and the bracketed entablature over each doorway. The 1836 Greek Revival dwelling at No. 463 was the first house built on the street, and belonged to a teacher at the Seminary. Look for the fine rope molding around the doorway at No. 455 and the pineapples (symbols of hospitality) on the cast-iron railings at No. 453.

Stop at No. 443 and look across the street into the seminary quadrangle for a view of the 1836 Gothic Revival fieldstone **West Building**, the oldest surviving structure on the campus. Down the block at No. 407 a female head in brownstone peers over the arched doorway of the **Guardian Angel Convent**. No. 405, a splendid Italianate brownstone, appears very much the way it did in 1853 except for the entrance doors.

CH29 Just before the corner, stop to read the plaque describing the Chelsea Historic District. It is on the side of the **Royer-Wells House** at No. 401 (1831-1832), also numbered 183 Ninth Avenue, the second oldest house in the Historic District (the oldest is coming up soon).

With its pitched roof and dormer windows, the two-and-a-half-story corner house recalls a rural image. James N. Wells moved here in 1833 when he began working with Clement Clarke Moore on developing the Chelsea estate. Wells used the dwelling as a home and office for two years and then moved to his newly built mansion at 414 West 22nd Street, keeping an office here for some time. In 1835 the ground floor was converted to a grocery store and the upstairs kept as living quarters.

Cross Ninth Avenue to the southeast corner of West 21st Street.

CH30 Wells owned the blockfront on the west side of Ninth Avenue from West 21st Street to West 22nd Street and in the 1840s erected three tiny, two-story wooden buildings next door at **Nos. 185, 187, and 189**. The corner house and the adjoining wooden building at No. 185 were acquired in 1993 and converted (Stephen B. Jacobs) to a private residence with a secluded back garden. The storefronts of all but No. 185 have been retained and a French cafe presently occupies the ground floor of the corner house. Look up at the brick wall of No. 191, facing the wooden houses, where traces of painted signage advertising the James N. Wells Company are visible.

Cross back to the west side of Ninth Avenue. Walk mid-block between West 21st and West 20th Streets.

CH31 The brick and stone main building of the **General Theological Seminary** at 175 Ninth Avenue (O'Connor & Kilham, 1960) replaces three distinguished Collegiate Gothic buildings from the original plan. A mixed-use facility, the building houses offices, a dean's residence, and the St. Mark's Library with its collection of ecclesiastical books. While the Library is available only to seminarians, scholars, and clergy, the grounds of the Seminary are open to the public Monday through Friday, noon to 3:00 P.M. and Saturday, 11:00 A.M. to 3:00 P.M. Entrance is through this building. Walk into the lobby and request a map of the campus. Be sure to look for the Chapel of the Good Shepherd with its handsome bronze doors and tympanum above the entrance illustrating scenes from the New Testament (J. Massey Rhind). If

Exit the seminary.
Walk south on
Ninth Avenue.
Cross West 20th
Street. Turn right
and walk to the
first row house.

you are visiting when the grounds are closed to the
public, ask if you may look through the glass doors into
the grassy quadrangle. You will be able to see the English Collegiate Gothic buildings that surround the grassy
lawns and venerable trees. The Seminary, one of the
hidden treasures of Manhattan, is not to be missed.

*The General
Theological Seminary,
looking west from the
Ninth Avenue elevated
railway, 1913. Three
Collegiate Gothic
structures were razed
for the 1960 main
buiding. At right, the
Royer-Wells House*

CH32 The houses on Chelsea Square South face the campus of the Seminary, which can be seen through the iron
fence. The oldest house in the Chelsea Historic District
stands at **No. 404**. Completed in 1830, the small Federal
house has been considerably altered over the years. An
original clapboard wall survives, visible on the east side
of the house. In the Greek Revival make-over, the doorway was remodeled with wooden pilasters, an upper
story topped by a modillioned cornice was added, and
the decorative wrought-iron railing was installed. Later,
parlor-floor windows were altered in the Italianate style.

Standing in the Historic District, the house is now protected by law from inappropriate changes.

CH33 **No. 402** (C.P.H. Gilbert, 1897) is a narrow Classical Revival apartment house with a curved facade. Chelsea insiders know that the letters over the doorway, "DONAC," honor a prominent neighborhood real estate developer, Don Alonzo Cushman. Cushman, an eighth-generation descendant of a prominent Puritan family, made a fortune in the dry goods business. He was associated with Clement Clarke Moore and James N. Wells in organizing the Church of St. Luke-in-the-Fields in Greenwich Village and in the development of property in Chelsea. Cushman's legacy is an architectural treasure, the Greek Revival row just down the block to the west.

CH34 **Cushman Row** (1839-1840) at Nos. 406-418 is regarded as one of the finest Greek Revival rows in the nation. In New York it is second only to the row on Washington Square North (1832-1833). The gracious red-brick houses with brownstone bases and a unified cornice line are set back behind ten-foot front yards framed by decorative iron railings.

Entrances are typical of the Greek Revival style. Brownstone pilasters supporting a horizontal entablature

Cushman Row, 406-418 West 20th Street between Ninth and Tenth Avenues, 1905. While each of the seven houses is notable, together they form a handsome urban vista.

The rear of the Cushman House facing the garden. On the veranda, the widow of Don Alonzo Cushman, Matilda Ritter Cushman, who died in 1881.

Begin walking west.

frame the single-paneled door topped by a transom and flanked by sidelights. Original cast-iron laurel wreaths encircle the attic windows of all but two of the houses (various dormers were added later). The wrought-iron yard railings with designs derived from Greek motifs are especially fine. Note the anthemion cresting, Greek key at the base, and graceful lyres in the gates. A plaque on No. 412 tells the story of Cushman Row. Elaborate cast-iron newel posts at No. 416 and No. 418 are topped by pineapple finials.

If you were unable to explore the Seminary grounds, cross West 20th Street for a good look at the cloistered campus through the iron fence.

Return to the southwest corner of Ninth Avenue and West 20th Street.

CH35 The spacious Greek Revival house on the southeast corner at **162 Ninth Avenue**, built in 1834, was the home of James N. Wells from 1842 to 1854.

CH36 In 1833 on the block facing the Seminary, at **9 Chelsea Square** (renumbered 170 Ninth Avenue) Don Alonzo Cushman built a large, four-story red-brick mansion with a porch of Colonial design, as well as an adjoining two-room office. A 400-foot garden in back of the house ran the width of the entire block and held a summer house, coach houses, and stables. The buildings were razed after the death of the Cushmans' eldest son in 1894.

CH37 A row of narrow Anglo-Italianate houses (1853-

1854) at **Nos. 358-348** was built for the children of James N. Wells.

Cushman House entrance hall, ca. 1880.

CH38 a-b Rising 130 feet mid-block on the south side of West 20th Street between Eighth and Ninth Avenues is the square tower of **St. Peter's Church** (James W. Smith,1836-1838). The Episcopal church is the centerpiece of a complex of three buildings. To the west at **No. 346** is the small, brick Greek Revival Chapel (1831-1832) which became the rectory in 1841. Its original design was sketched by Clement Clarke Moore. The church was also intended to be in the Greek Revival style until, as the story goes, a vestryman brought back a drawing of Magdalen College, Oxford. Plans were changed and St. Peter's became the first English parish Gothic church in America. It was constructed by an architect-builder, and supervised by Moore. With its rough stone exterior and heavy buttresses, the building looks indestructible, but the tower has lost its pinnacles and Gothic Revival porches, and has been undergoing major repairs for the past 50 years. Chelsea Community Church shares the church with the Episcopal congregation.

Cross Ninth Avenue and West 20th Street. Walk east on the north side of West 20th Street.

Walk to the middle of the block.

To the east of the church at **No. 336** is the former Parish Hall (1871), a red-brick Victorian Gothic structure with lancet windows and a crenelated tower. It is now occupied by the Atlantic Theater Company, founded in Chicago in 1985 by David Mamet and William H. Macy. The award-winning acting ensemble produces new American plays at their playhouse in Vermont and in this desanctified church building.

Notice the iron gates and simple wrought-iron fence fronting all three buildings. The railings date from the 1790s and once stood in front of Trinity Church on lower Broadway. In a link with the past that Moore must

St. Peter's Episcopal Church, 1903. At right, the Greek Revival Chapel. The Parish Hall is to the left.

132

have appreciated, since his father had been a rector at Trinity, St. Peter's was given the fence in 1837 when work began on the present building of the downtown church.

CH39 On the southwest corner of West 19th Street is the former Elgin Theater (Simon Zelnik, 1942). Today it is the exuberant Art Moderne **Joyce Theater** (renovations, Hardy, Holzman, Pfeiffer Associates, 1981-1982), the shining star of Eighth Avenue. Established by Eliot Feld and the Original Ballets Foundation, the internationally acclaimed center for dance has been stunningly renovated as a performance space. The neighborhood movie house was redesigned with a facade animated by patterned brick and with glass brick framing the entrance. The 474-seat theater is named in honor of the late daughter of LuEsther Mertz, a major patron of dance. The Joyce Theater ranks as one of the nation's preeminent cultural sites for the production and performance of dance. Since its opening in 1982, audiences have flocked here for performances by such stellar dance companies as Merce Cunningham, Erick Hawkins, Alwin Nikolais, and the Feld Ballets.

Continue walking on West 20th Street to Eighth Avenue. Turn right and walk to the southwest corner of West 19th Street.

The Joyce Theater sparked a cultural revival of the neighborhood. Eighth Avenue is now a restaurant row and the theater scene in Chelsea is thriving. Hudson Guild Theater has had the longest run, presenting dramas since 1922. The WPA Theatre, Atlantic Theater Company, and Actor's Theatre Workshop offer varied productions. The Irish Repertory, Repertorio Español, and American Jewish Theater have their respective niches. The Vortex Theater Group presents works by gay and lesbian playwrights in the Sanford Meisner Theater. Dance Theater Workshop is a pioneer in modern dance, showcasing lesser known dancers, and the Kitchen is an avantgarde mixed-media performance space. Alive with other performance groups, live-music rooms, and dance clubs, Chelsea is making a comeback, recalling its earlier years as a major entertainment center of the city.

Relax in one of the many restaurants or cafes along Eighth Avenue.

Acknowledgments

My list of acknowledgements begins with Jane R. Crotty, former Executive Director of the 23rd Street Association, Inc. and present Director of Community Relations and Economic Development at Baruch College (CUNY) whose enthusiasm and know-how propelled this project forward. I am deeply indebted to Peg Breen, President of the New York Landmarks Conservancy, for her steadfast involvement and gracious support. My heartfelt gratitude to Margot Gayle, legendary preservation activist and author, for her scrutiny of the text and perceptive observations. And special thanks to my partner, Marvin Berman, who walked along with me in the neighborhoods and through the pages of this guide, offering astute comments and unfailing encouragement.

I appreciate the efforts of Roger P. Lang, the Conservancy's Director of Community Programs and Services, the work of Peter S. Pockriss, the Conservancy's Director of Development, Tara N. Sullivan, indefatigable photo researcher and editorial assistant, and Jennifer A. Wellock, research assistant. To Mary Shapiro, Kimber VanRy, and Joe Zito who, along with others, read the manuscript and provided thoughtful commentary, I offer profound thanks. In the transformation of manuscript into book, I was fortunate to be able to rely on the technical assistance of my son Eric D. Mendelsohn, the skillful copy-editing of Tim Holahan, and the creative design team of Abraham Brewster and Ron Gordon of The Oliphant Press.

The Designation Reports of the New York City Landmarks Preservation Commission have provided invaluable information on the historic districts and individual landmarks. The research of Andrew Dolkart and Christopher Gray, architectural historians and Richard McDermott, publisher of the New York Chronicle, has been especially helpful. I gratefully acknowledge the assistance of Kenneth Cobb, Director of the Municipal Archives; Daniel May, Archivist, MetLife Archives; Lucille Romano and Bob Houston of the Consolidated Edison Company

of New York; Eileen Kennedy, Museum of the City of
New York; Ronald Cohen, Archivist, Appellate Division,
Supreme Court of New York, and the staff of the Local
History Division of the New York Public Library,
Municipal Reference Library, and Library of the New-
York Historical Society.

Individuals who have shared their knowledge and
insights with me include: Tom Agnew, New York City
Department of Design and Construction. Thomas S.
Arbuckle, International Toy Center. Sharen Benenson,
Trustee, Gramercy Park. Margie Berk, preservationist.
Irene Bradkey, St. Mark's Library, General Theological
Seminary. Richard Bonnabeau, Archivist, Empire State
College. Lawrence Campbell, Archivist, Art Students
League. Sally Campbell, Friends House in Rosehill. Paul
Custer, Executive Director, McBurney Y.M.C.A. Robert
Daniels, Joyce Theater. Harriet Davis-Kram, historian.
Don De Franco, Vice President, Stribling-Wells & Gay.
Patty Dugan, Douglas Elliman. The Reverend Stephen
Garmey, Vicar, Cavalry Church. Marvin Gelfand, urban
historian. Val Ginter, urban historian. Steven S. Grant,
Masonic Hall. Chris Huff, New York Life Insurance Co.
Lauren Kaplan, Chelsea Piers. Jeffrey Kroessler, histo-
rian. Zev Lazar, Director, New York City Department of
Citywide Administrative Services. Rabbi Meyer Leifer,
Congregation Emunath Israel. Missia Leonard, Director,
Historic Preservation Office, New York City Department
of Design and Construction. Erwin Levold, Rockefeller
Archives Center. Walter Mankoff, U.N.I.T.E. Charles
Markis, Director, Theodore Roosevelt Birthplace
National Historic Site. Dorothea McElduff, Church of
Our Guardian Angel. Deborah S. McWilliams, MetLife.
Kate Milkens, New York City Department of Parks &
Recreation. William D. Moore, Director, Livingston
Masonic Library. Barry Moreno, Statue of Liberty Foun-
dation. Tom O'Brien, General Manager, Gramercy Park
Hotel. Loren Pack, ABC Carpet & Home. John Panter,
Parish Historian, Trinity Church. Jennie Prebor, Dia
Center for the Arts. Candace Pryor, Archivist, Y.M.C.A.
of Greater New York. Michael Quercia, Archival Assis-
tant, Educational and Cultural Trust Fund of the Electri-

cal Industry. Sandra Roff, Archivist, Baruch College. Kenneth J. Ross, Research Librarian, Presbyterian Church (U.S.A.). Peter Salwen, President, Salwen Communications. John Simoudis, The Inn at Irving Place. Sheldon C. Silberstein, transit historian. Diana Stevens, Assistant Director Public Affairs, United Synagogue of Conservative Judaism. Jack Taylor, preservation activist. June Taylor, John F. Kennedy Library. Robert Trentlyon, Chelsea Waterside Park Association. Susan Tobin, Archivist, Congregation Shearith Israel. Susan Tunick, President, Friends of Terra Cotta. Sharon Ullman, Executive Director, 23rd St. Association, Inc. Jean Seward Uppman. Angela Vega, Archivist, New York Life Insurance Co. Jerry Weinstein, General Manager, Chelsea Hotel. Raymond Wemmlinger, Curator and Librarian, Hampden-Booth Theatre Library, The Players.

Index to Tours

Selected Bibliography

Baral, Robert. Turn West on 23rd Street: A Toast to New York's Old Chelsea. NY: Fleet Publishing Corp, 1965.

Benjamin, Marcus. A Historical Sketch of Madison Square. NY: Meridian Britannia Co., 1894.

Boyer, M. Christine. Manhattan Manners: Architecture and Style 1850-1900. NY: Rizzoli, 1985.

Dreiser, Theodore. Sister Carrie. NY: Doubleday, 1900.

Dodge, Henry Irving. Forty Years on Twenty-Third Street. NY: The Garfield National Bank, 1923.

Dolkart, Andrew Scott. Gramercy. Its Architectural Surroundings. NY: Gramercy Neighborhood Associates, Inc., 1996.

Garmey, Stephen. Gramercy Park: An Illustrated History of a New York Neighborhood. NY: Balsam Press, 1984.

Gayle, Margot and Michele Cohen. The Art Commission and the Municipal Art Society Guide to Manhattan's Outdoor Sculpture. NY: Prentice Hall Press, 1988.

Hendrickson, Robert. The Grand Emporiums: The Illustrated History of America's Great Department Stores. NY: Stein & Day, 1979.

Landau, Sarah Bradford and Carl W. Condit. Rise of the New York Skyscraper 1865-1913. New Haven: Yale University Press, 1996.

Lockwood, Charles. Bricks and Brownstone, The New York Rowhouse 1783-1929. NY: Abbeville Press, 1972.
    Manhattan Moves Uptown. Boston: Houghton Mifflin Co., 1976.

Lowe, David Garrard. Stanford White's New York. NY: Doubleday, 1992.

Horowitz, Paul J., editor. O. Henry, Collected Stories. NY: Dorset Press, 1994.

New York City Landmarks Preservation Commission.
    Chelsea Historic District Designation Report (1970) Extension (1981)
    Gramercy Park Historic District Designation Report (1966) Extension (1988)
    Ladies' Mile Historic District Designation Report (1989)

Patterson, Samuel White. Old Chelsea & St. Peter's Church. NY: Friebele Press, 1935.

Stallman, R.W. and E.R,. Hagemann. The New York City Sketches of Stephen Crane. NY: New York University Press, 1966.

Wharton, Edith. A Backward Glance. NY: Charles Scribner's Sons, 1933.
    The Age of Innocence. NY: D. Appleton and Co., 1920.

Wolfe, Gerard R. New York, A Guide to the Metropolis. NY: McGraw Hill, Inc., 1994.

Illustration Sources

Archives and Libraries

Appellate Division, Supreme Court of New York State: p. 22

Collection of The New-York Historical Society: pp. 28, 29, 33, 38, 42, 45, 47, 51, 52, 55, 57, 59, 60, 74, 77, 78, 81, 83, 90, 91, 102, 112, 114, 122, 123, 129, 131

Consolidated Edison Company of New York: cover, pp. 20, 53, 54

dialogboxnyc: p. 66

The General Theological Seminary of the Episcopal Church: pp. 125, 128

Livingston Masonic Library: p. 82

The MetLife Archives: pp. 10, 12, 18, 23, 32

Mutual Redevelopment Houses: p. 110

The Museum of the City of New York: pp. 16, 19, 49, 61, 79, 80, 81, 85, 95, 97, 98, 99, 101, 109, 115, 117, 130

The New York Public Library, Manuscripts and Archives Division, United States History, Local History and Genealogy Division: pp. 8, 30, 51, 63, 67, 71, 72, 93

New York Life Insurance Company: p. 27

St. Peter's Episcopal Church: p. 132

Theodore Roosevelt Birthplace National Historic Site: p. 36

UPI Bettman Archives: pp. 44, 77, 86, 107, 113, 118